CRISIS to COMEBACK

A roadmap to health transformation after burnout

Crisis to Comeback: A roadmap to health transformation after burnout

First Printing, 2023

ISBN: 978-1-7393877-1-6 Published by: Maria Fox

Publisher Web address: www.livewellandfree.co.uk

Cover design by: Maria Fox

Editor: Tracey Taylor: music@traceytaylor.co.uk

Book Interior and E-book Design by Amit Dey | amitdey2528@gmail.com

Table of Contents

Dedications

To the One who gives me breath and whose grace, favour and provision in my life has led me to a new understanding of what it means to live life to the full.

To Jenny, Steve, Vanessa, Sam, Sara, and Jane who have walked with me for many years as the best of friends – thank you for showing incredible patience, kindness, love, and loyalty through the most incredibly testing time in my life.

To Lumen co-founders Michal and Merav Tor and CEOs Daniel Tal and Dror Ceder - thank you for pursuing your mission to help others navigate a path to metabolic health – I will be forever grateful for your dedication, diligence, and determination. Lumen has changed my life forever and I know it has the potential to change millions more!

To Annie Grace – thank you for sharing your journey and how you changed your relationship with alcohol. Thank you for developing an approach for countless others to follow and break free from its suffocating hold without shame or blame, by removing the desire to drink alcohol in the first place.

Disclaimer

The views, approaches, use of biometric and metabolic devices described in this narrative, specifically Lumen and Garmin Fenix are personal to the author and do not represent any views, endorsement or promotion by West Midlands Police or policing per se.

Endorsements

All that you are about to read and assimilate in this book, we have watched Maria discover, absorb, and walk out for herself up close. This is more than a testimony of someone's journey of recovery, it is also a manual and guide, full of proven facts, truths and principles that can truly transform your life, starting from the inside out. We celebrate Maria's accomplishments, both in the restoration of health, but this first publication too! As you deep dive into this, you certainly will not be disappointed!

Stephen and Jenny Watson

Leaders – Kingdom Advance Network and forever friends of Maria

Maria's courage in sharing her journey provides us all with a stark reminder that health and well-being is an incredibly unique phenomenon comprising of a complex array of issues from early life experiences, faith, and gender through to diet, nutrition and sleep. Her book captures this beautifully with humour and humility allowing the reader to find their own path by learning from the experiences of another. All too often we are encouraged to think there is a quick fix to workforce health and well-being or that a one size fits all approach can sheep dip us into a better, healthier life. In her book Maria reminds us of the uniqueness of our mental and physical health so that we can think more deeply about the issues she covers

Andy Rhodes

Director of Oscar Kilo National Police Well-being

Maria started her well-being recovery supported by her newly purchased lumen device, something which we know as the founders/developers, holds important keys to metabolic health. Her subsequent use of her lumen metabolic feedback, nutrition plans and insights propelled her towards a flexible metabolism and healthy lifestyle which far exceeded her expectations. As developers of this innovative technology to improve metabolic health, sustained weight loss, improved sleep and overall wellness, we are excited that not only has Maria's journey validated so much that we knew was true from a scientific perspective, but it has also evidenced what is absolutely within the grasp of so many if they are willing to take the right approach for them to the pillars of sleep, mindset/stress management, nutrition and exercise. It has been wonderful watching Maria's transformation but also the leadership and inspiration she has provided for others in the ever-growing Lumen Facebook community as our lead group expert. Her book tells the story of what's possible, inspiring, and equipping the reader to take hold of their own health in a practical, yet insightful way.

Daniel Tal
CEO, Lumen

Maria describes an honest account of her turnaround moment in this book "Crisis to Comeback". Alcohol, early menopause, the stress of police work and just everyday life had begun to write a convincing narrative for Maria - her LIFE was finished. However, she was able to stop, take advice, set some new goals, and find herself again. Many of us can recognize this crossroads too, feeling that we are hardly surviving let alone thriving. Let this book encourage you to take some first steps… and then the rest is history as they say!

Rachel Hickson
Author and Director of Heartcry

I met Maria on the 11th of July 1994 - the day we both joined policing nearly 30 years ago now. It's been quite a journey! Two people who couldn't be more different formed a life-long bond. The extrovert and the introvert ploughing similar paths through policing, passionate about delivering the very best service possible to communities and keeping a constant eye out for one another along the way.

In this book Maria credits a conversation we had when she was at her lowest. The credit however goes entirely to Maria. Being able to recognise herself at her lowest ebb and return to the position she is today flying high with energy, passion and drive has been a delight to see.

This book describes how, with an understanding of the simple pillars of sleep, mindset/stress management, nutrition, and exercise, (pillars available to everyone), we can all become our true selves and live a fulfilled and happy life. The frankness with which Maria describes where she had got too is refreshing. Her journey is one many will be able to relate to, but perhaps not see themselves achieving the same success. This book will show that you can become whatever you set your mind to; it is possible, and Maria will describe how.

I am proud of the way Maria has turned her life around and very proud to call her my friend.

Vanessa Jardine
Chief Constable, Northumbria Police

I first met Maria in 1997 at a promotion process, I liked her from the start, smart, funny, passionate about policing, hardworking, energetic, compassionate, and ethical to the core, exactly what you want in a police officer. I have very fond memories of us both as Detective Sergeants comparing what we had to deal with in the custody block, Maria was working on an inner-city Manchester division, and I was at Southampton Central, so I always found the calls very reassuring as my day ahead was never as bad as Maria's! We progressed through our policing careers, mainly in CID roles, and Maria always gave 100% to every role with humility and genuine concern for her fellow colleagues and the public always at the fore. During 2020, I received a phone call to say that Maria was off work long term sick; the colleague who called was a bit sheepish about the reasons for her absence so I knew immediately it would be stress and burn out. Policing takes its toll on individuals and the service is often the scapegoat for failing politicians, policies or the latest social ill; the pressure is relentless and can leave its mark physically, emotionally, and spiritually. Most of us rely on caffeine to wake us up, sugar to keep us going, alcohol to wind down and once we hit our mid-forties (especially as women going though hormonal chaos) it gets a lot harder to maintain and habits that used to serve us no longer do.

I contacted Maria immediately I heard the news, and we spent hours discussing the latest research and trading experiences. I feel genuinely privileged to have been part of Maria's health journey, and to witness her 'bounce back' with her usual levels of exceptional enthusiasm, with every facet of health and wellbeing explored. Maria didn't just want solutions she wanted to understand what was going on in her body, why it had happened and how to recover, using any 'bio hack' she assessed as relevant. Alongside her quest for her own health came the drive to share her lived experience in the hope that it would resonate with others and help them to solve their own health puzzles, particularly those who give their body, heart, and soul, in the service of others. Not satisfied with merely delivering presentations, she quickly embarked on her journey as an author to share the breadth and depth of all aspects in her determination to speak into organisational cultures and exhort people towards better self-care and improved health and wellbeing. Her book achieves that with humour, transparency, courage, and clarity.

Sara Glen
Naturopathic Nutritionist, CEO Infinite8Wellbeing,
former Deputy Chief Constable, Hampshire Constabulary

While browsing the Lumen Facebook community, I discovered Maria Fox and was impressed by her dedication to helping others achieve a successful health journey. As a health and physical education teacher in Australian schools for over three decades, I've garnered a substantial following for my health podcast, spanning across 93 countries. Maria's unwavering support for individuals within the group caught my attention, and I was drawn to her authenticity. Her book about health aligns with my criteria for a relatable and inspiring example, and I believe it is a valuable investment for anyone looking to improve their overall well-being.

Shane Stubbs
Bachelor of Health and Physical Education 1988
Outsmart classroom and Podcast host

Foreword

By Annie Grace of *This Naked Mind* and Chief Constable Lisa Winward, from North Yorkshire Police

As the founder of This Naked Mind,[1] I've had the privilege of watching Maria's amazing journey and transformation, from being a member of my community, to mentor and now a Certified Coach. It's a deep-spirited story of perseverance and tenacity, about a lady who refused to give up and accept a set of very challenging circumstances.

Life is an incredible journey. I am convinced our responsibility as humans, is to take care of and respect each other and this planet, which is our home. But, in order to do that, we must first take care of and respect ourselves. We must love ourselves first, take care of ourselves, change our habits and our behaviours and only then we can change the world. This is exactly what Maria decided to do.

I have no doubt that her words will be an inspiration to anyone who needs to call 'time-out' for the sake of their health and well-being; those who are grappling with stress, overwhelm, burn-out, trauma, or addiction. Maria is living proof that each of us can navigate the toughest of paths, to find compassion for ourselves, change our behaviours and ultimately change our entire life.

In her deeply personal and vulnerable account, Maria credits the organisations that have helped and supported her along the way. However, I must say – all credit must go to Maria. Without her courage and deep well of motivation, this story would have ended quite differently. Instead, it is an ode to self-love, self-care and self-discovery.

Take heart and enjoy.

Love, Annie Grace.
(CEO of This Naked Mind and author of the books: *This Naked Mind – Control Alcohol: Find Freedom, Discover Happiness & Change Your Life*; *The Alcohol Experiment*; and co-author with William Porter of *This Naked Mind: Nicotine*)

✣ ✣ ✣

Joining the police is like joining an institution, where we are the people who are called upon day and night to help others who are, at times, in severe crisis; things that most people couldn't even imagine in their worst nightmares. What this sometimes creates is a sense of 'superhero', where we cannot be weak or broken ourselves and we hide it well – until it is too late. What is needed, is for our 'superheroes' to feel their own vulnerability and be able to share it so that other people can have permission to share their vulnerabilities, too.

Maria has done just that and the first time I encountered her was watching a recording of her story in a presentation. When I switched it on, I thought I would just watch the first few minutes. But her story was so compelling that I could not stop myself from watching the entire presentation…and how much better I felt for doing so.

Maria's book covers first-hand experience of what happens when things become too much and, in Maria's case, the additional context of the peri-menopause. She describes how the combination of different toxic factors can conspire so profoundly, to be detrimental to every aspect of our lives. Despite this, Maria's story is one of hope as she digs deep into root causes, signposting the reader to 'prevention' as well as 'cure'. She shares simple, yet effective tactics to improve overall health and in the case of burnout and fatigue, a road map to recover well in the face of such a setback. Her story is truly inspirational.

Lisa Winward.
(Chief Constable, N. Yorkshire Police)

Preface

I have been motivated to write this book following what felt like a total catastrophe health-wise, workwise, fitness-wise and life-wise and, because, against all odds, I turned the adversity into opportunity. I want to share with you my journey back to optimal health and well-being to encourage you to make yours a priority, too. I hope the insights that I pass on are an example of how you can navigate towards improved physical and mental health, presenting more beneficial ways of managing stress, workload and all the wide-ranging demands placed upon you.

My crisis experience was 'a moment in time', as my appointed counsellor Henrietta Hutton Potts often reminded me. Those reassuring words still call out powerfully to me even now, carrying a deep sense of resonance. It's a phrase with which I continue to encourage others with, knowing that in those initial moments following the white flag of surrender, when all you feel is loss, grief and hopelessness; where your career, your health and your state of mind feel in tatters, and it seems as though everything is crashing down around you… It's in those moments when you're faced with dead end after dead end, with no navigation system to help you find your way out of the maze, when you need to remember – it is a moment in time. You *will* come out the other side.

So... here I was, nearing the end of what had so far been an amazing career and vocation in the UK police service, feeling as though I was done. The encroaching fear that I had lost all capability and capacity to do my job was looming in the near distance. My dream of achieving all I had aspired to be as a leader in policing was fading. It had eluded me, leaving me with an awareness of deep disappointment that I would now finish my career with regret, instead of fulfilment. The sense of satisfaction and achievement that I had hoped for in fulfilling my potential as a senior policing leader, was slipping away and out of my grasp. Disappointment, bewilderment, frustration, helplessness, anger and confusion were just some of the emotions I felt at the beginning of my transformation journey. Retrospectively of course, I can call it a transformation journey. However, at the time it felt as though I had fallen into a black hole. I was contemplating early retirement options because I could not see, nor did I believe, that I could turn this situation around; it all felt so irredeemable.

However, a little less than four years out from thirty years' police service, retirement did not present the most financially viable option. How was I ever going to be well enough to do my job to the best of my ability again? I had no clue...Yet in the days, weeks and months that followed I began to navigate a path that would see me not only recover, but transform my health – mentally, physically and emotionally – to become the best and healthiest version of me [to date]. Additionally, I would find a new vision to inspire, lead and teach others how to achieve the same, without the need for a crash and burn experience to prompt action.

I hope my story encourages and emboldens you to believe that you can make changes, little by little, which will enable you to be the best version of yourself that you can be, for you to become an author of your future, rather than falling prey to a false destiny. You are unique – there is only one you. No replica, no mistake. You are uniquely created for purpose and destiny, different to me and every other human being on planet earth. This means you'll need to navigate your path according to your own circumstances. However, like me, you can learn to take control of the things that you are able to, and by so doing, find your highway to happiness in making your life count. Make every moment your happiest, for those you love and for those whom you serve.

Introduction

In the pages that follow, I share some of my life journey with you, giving particular focus on the latter few years from which this book, "From Crisis to Comeback," originated. In it I share the highs, the lows, what I have learned about myself and about life, about health, examining what's important and what isn't. I also share ideas and put forward suggestions for further reading, which you will find at the back. You will also find a link to my website, which contains some helpful tools and hopefully, in the very near future, there will also be a downloadable guide available relating to what I call my "Four Pillars," namely Nutrition, Movement, Sleep and Stress/mindset Management.

At the beginning of my recovery journey, my physical statistics were not good. My body mass index [BMI] was 30.5; I weighed in at 210lb [14 stone 10lb] and I had a fat percentage of 35. To add to that, I had just suffered my second blood clot and was also displaying serious ECG irregularities. Probably more profoundly however, all these physical symptoms were manifestations of a nervous system under siege, with mental health having reached an all-time low – all significantly exacerbated by peri-menopausal hormone imbalance.

It is remarkable two years on to now report a BMI of 22.8, a consistent weight range of 149-153lb [10st 8-12], 'managed risk' in relation to blood clots and reversed health metrics in terms of my ECG. I am pleased to report a normal cardiac rhythm and the achievement of many personal and professional milestones in the last twelve months, ranging from coaching accreditations to operational policing re-accreditations, with a temporary promotion to the rank of Chief Superintendent.

When I look back on my policing career, I wonder, had I known what I know now regarding my knowledge of the Four Pillars, whether I might have navigated my path slightly differently. Why had I not taken the time to discover some real basics about health and well-being? Why did it take a crisis for me to wake up? How had I ended up on a path where alcohol had become the go-to medicine for just about every reason? How had it become so woven into the fabric of my life to become my stress relief and my reward? My celebration and my switching off? My companion on holiday and…dare I say, influenced by police culture? It had punctuated so many things that in the end, my brain pretty much connected it with most of life's experiences. It had become normal and necessary. It is in the chapter *Alcohol: Friend or Foe* where I delve into this extensively.

Was my constant rush a smokescreen for deeper issues of self-worth and striving to prove myself all the time? I have asked myself so many questions. What I anticipated was that if I could get to my 50th birthday and have a holiday away from everything, it would all be OK. It was an optimistic thought! I share my thoughts concerning this in chapter 1 as some aspects may resonate with you, enabling you to reflect on your own journey, encouraging you to seek support before ending up where I did.

In this book, I will walk you through the many discoveries I made day by day, week by week and month by month, as I sought to take control of my Four Pillars. I will share with you the keys that I have identified from a personal growth and resilience perspective, alongside the pillars, to optimise physical and mental health.

The truth is, when we are the healthiest version of ourselves and we take care of ourselves well, we are able to give, live and perform to the highest standard. Some may think self-care is for "softies" and is akin to some kind of sycophantic pursuit. But the reality is, if YOUR cup is empty, you cannot truly give to anyone else, or serve anyone else. However, if YOUR cup is full, and you keep refilling it, you have plenty to give day after day.

Learning to say "no" has been one of the hardest lessons for me to learn. Feeling more comfortable saying "no," has also taken time. Feeling the fear of judgement looming, I realise that people have felt I've let them down. However, I am learning to be responsible for the load I can bear instead of taking responsibility for how others might react.

My personal growth as a leader has been greatly accelerated by the amazing training that I received with *This Naked Mind Institute* (TNMI)[2], with whom I am now an accredited coach. Additionally, I have advanced as a result of my role within the fast-growing *Lumen*[3] health community, where I am now a lead group expert and metabolic coach.

Discovering the Four Pillars alongside my professional and personal development of goal setting, sharpening focus skills, learning to prioritise and implement action plans, have all helped me to achieve more in the last twelve months than possibly the last decade. That might be the subject of another book. In the pages of this book, I will offer the best practical advice that I can, to help you and your loved ones navigate towards better health and well-being.

1

That Sunday Afternoon

Sunday 25th October 2020 will be forever etched in my memory, just as the 11th of July 1994, when I donned a police uniform for the first time. I will never forget that Sunday evening… It had been a miserable afternoon, a typical damp and grey English autumnal day. I was sitting alone in my lounge wondering what on earth was going on in my life, questioning why I was feeling so low and seemingly unable to move forward. As evening came, I found myself staring bleary-eyed at an empty wine bottle, desperately trying to figure out how I had arrived at this place. My thoughts turned towards a second flagon in a bid to numb out the reality of what I imagined lay ahead…

I recognised something was very wrong and equally knew the wine I was downing was simply a momentary soul-mate. As someone facing multiple medical health conditions, this made my relationship with alcohol a doubly worrying concept. Alongside my medical issues, the lingering injuries I had sustained from a previous bike accident were also really taking their toll on me. All-in-all, the additional strain to my already fragile mental and emotional health was beginning to approach danger level.

I was experiencing, what I now understand with hindsight, the spectra of symptoms associated with burnout, fatigue and breakdown, brought on by multiple and complex factors, (which I unpack in a future chapter).

I was experiencing extreme emotional dysfunction. I had a sense of being totally overwhelmed, coupled with the awareness of not being able to cope anymore with any aspect of life. Usually a very positive "glass half-full" person, it seemed as though life, as I had known it, was slipping away in front of my eyes, and I was being drawn, uncontrollably, into the void of a black hole…

The onset of peri-menopausal symptoms was beginning to hit me hard. The thing is, many of these symptoms are like the signs of burnout and fatigue, so it was hard to differentiate initially what was causing what. Brain fog, the 'emotional roller-coaster' syndrome, forgetfulness, the inability to concentrate, depression, feelings of anxiety and low mood, all made me feel as though my cognitive ability was diminishing and I would never be able to do my job or be successful at anything again. It sounds overly dramatic as I write, and so far, removed from who I am now, to be barely believable. Yet in those moments of despair, it is exactly how I felt. Tearful at anything and everything. Zero emotional resilience and my tank was well and truly on empty.

Understandably, my self-image reached an all-time low. I hated how I looked, avoided being included in any photo opportunities and whilst relatively fit, as I had been during most of my life, I had once again ballooned to 14 stone 10lb, tipping myself into the Obese category. I had hit rock bottom. I looked and felt fat and was yet another statistic putting pressure on the health service. I loathed going shopping for clothes as it was more evidence of failure that I couldn't even manage my weight, let alone anything else in my life. I was under a cardiologist for Supraventricular Tachycardia,[4] a hematologist for my deep vein thrombosis and I was on a waiting list to see a private menopause specialist in relation to the acute symptoms I was experiencing.

As I sat and looked at the empty wine bottle, I began to sob uncontrollably. I can't remember whether it was me who called my long-time police colleague and friend, Vanessa, or whether she called me, but in our discourse that night she spoke words I needed to hear. Vanessa had been with me on my policing journey since day one and was without doubt a Godsend. She knew I wasn't well – she had been trying to tell me for weeks...but stubborn old me wasn't ready to face the truth. During one of our conversations, I broke down. Vanessa responded frankly, "You really need to take time out, Maria. You aren't yourself – this isn't you... You aren't very well. You need some time off."

"Yeh" I replied, "I am going to take a rest day in lieu[5] tomorrow."

"I am not talking about a rest day in lieu," contended Vanessa, "I am talking about you reporting sick."

I knew she was right. I knew things needed to change. I knew that if I didn't call time out now, it might be too late. I was in danger of stepping beyond a point of no return, of crossing an irreversible threshold and losing myself altogether. If I wanted to recover my purpose, meaning and destiny, I needed to listen to and act upon my friend's advice. Every day, for much of the preceding months that led up to our conversation, I had been waking at 4 am gripped with anxiety and regret, unable to get back to sleep. Filled with a sense of failure, my mind would replay over and over the missed opportunities... How I'd let others down, how I'd not been the best I could have been and the regret of using alcohol to switch off from it all. The vicious cycle was beginning to form around me again, giving rise to feelings of being imprisoned in a toxic pattern where there was no way out.

We finished our phone call and I returned to the lounge. I sat and stared into space, re-visiting aspects of our conversation. I trusted Vanessa implicitly. She had always been there for me, even when our working roles were in different force areas. She always talked sense and as I reflected on what my next steps needed to be; this occasion was no different. I turned to my best friend Jenny for a second opinion, who concurred with what Vanessa had said: I needed to take a break. I finally raised the white flag of surrender. My question now was, how should I report sick? *What* would I report sick *with*? After all, I didn't have a broken leg or the flu... And what action could I take in order to push back what felt like a tidal wave about to wipe me out?

I did manage to make one decision that night, a choice that would have an immediate impact on my health, and that was, until I could differentiate what was causing what, alcohol consumption had to be not just restricted but completely removed. At least that way I could focus and narrow down the different aspects that needed addressing, to see if I actually could get better. I knew that the first fourteen days of detox might be challenging, from previously undertaking Annie Grace's *This Naked Mind Intensive*[6] coaching programme in 2018. I also knew that once I'd made it through those first two weeks, I was over the worst of it.

One thing I have learnt from my plight is how much alcohol works as an aggravator and exaggerator in negative situations. For me, it distorted and exacerbated every problem I was facing. Too many of us have bought into the lies perpetrated by societal messaging and subliminal culture that tells us alcohol helps to relax, unwind, and de-stress. In my chapter '*Alcohol: Friend or Foe?*' the evidence suggests that it does anything but that.

As for me, I had finally seen the light and was not going to allow alcohol to dupe me ever again. Nevermore would I grant alcohol a foothold to present itself as an answer to my predicaments. I knew beyond the shadow of a doubt that eliminating it from the mix, would help bring into clear focus the real issues I was grappling with.

Incredibly, and to my surprise, it was the simplest detox. No cravings, no desire the next evening, not even the usual fourteen days of summoning will power! Assigning a curfew to week-day drinking in the preceding fortnight certainly had helped; however, perhaps more credit goes to the truth that I had finally woken up to the severity of where I now found myself. It was a big win in the midst of all the turmoil and misery I felt.

With this enlightenment, I was very quickly able to 'dig deep' and with the help of "The Live Alcohol Experiment[7]" I was soon motoring along with great momentum and ease.

Removing alcohol [and quickly losing any desire for it] proved to be the catalyst for taking control of so many other things in the days and weeks to come. It all felt very organic and unplanned, though looking back it's good to see there was a semblance of order. Step-by-step, each small decision I made helped me to gather momentum for the life-changing journey I had embarked upon.

So, what would be the first lesson I'd impart as a result of all I had learned thus far on this crossing? It would be to stop worrying about what people think of you. Stop seeking the approval of others and trying to please them in a way that compromises truth. It only adds anxiety and stress to your nervous system — which you do not need on top of the pressures within policing, or whatever job or situation you are in. What counts in life is that you love yourself, you love others, you do your best and accomplish what is required of you.

I confess to being the most grumpy, depressed and awful person to be around at times during my crisis, especially in those moments of reflecting on my personal attributes that I had taken for granted, knowing not how or when they might return. I remember setting about writing a list of all the things I could do to make myself better, ahead of my first counselling appointment and declaring to myself, "Perhaps I could get better with two weeks off work..." I chuckle now as I look back - thinking I could fix my nervous system within a fortnight! It had most definitely given me the thumbs down to coming back online anytime soon and I was swiftly to endure this reality. My operating system was about to reboot through the longest software update and hardware replacements I might ever experience!

2

Life in My Fast Lane

Reflecting now on my twenty-eight years of police service, I have loved pretty much every moment. I hold fond and treasured memories both of my early days in Greater Manchester as well as in my more recent service in the West Midlands.

I had real adventures on the front line, from commandeering mountain bikes, buses, and taxis in the pursuit of baddies, to stumbling upon drugs and firearms stashes, to executing warrants in the middle of the night (sometimes at the wrong flat number – ooops!). I vividly remember myself and a colleague receiving information from an informant about a drugs hoard, waking up the magistrate to obtain the warrant and forcing entry to the premises, only to find an elderly couple fast asleep in bed! (It was a multi-occupancy dwelling). We swiftly called the source to clarify the location and it turned out it was the residence on the right, not the left, by which time of course the drugs were down the toilet! It was moments like these, and so many more, which made life in policing so dynamic. There was never a monotonous moment, definitively playing into my appetite for adventure.

Walking my beat area (or "Bravo Beat" as it was in those days) included the 'Theatre of Dreams' (aka the Manchester United football stadium at Old Trafford), together with Lancashire County Cricket ground – two main focal points in Stretford. Rain, snow or shine, Inspector Otto would have his probationary constables out on foot patrol stopping cars, doing 'process'[8], CLE2/6's (expired vehicle excise duty), parking tickets, vehicle defects (with a mini competition to see who came back in with the most!), not to mention green cards[9] (summons reports), which were forever returned from the Sergeant with red pen ("re-write it please")! From being assaulted after a foot chase with a burglar, to apprehending a man with a samurai sword, my early policing days were filled with adventure – and I loved it.

As a fervent officer, I was keen to accelerate in both personal promotion and supporting others. I was absolutely thrilled when, upon completing my standard response car course,[10] I was asked to tutor a brand-new police officer. I was chuffed to have proven my overall operational abilities and skills, to have achieved part one of the Sergeant's exam and be already transitioning into the role of Detective. I was in the fast lane!

There were so many formative and unforgettable experiences in my early days with my fantastic and highly motivated team mates on 'A relief,'[11] – high-fives to Marina, Barney, Stuart and Glyn, to name but a few. They set the bar high for me in terms of my career aspirations. The promotion path was never in my mind when I joined the force, just foot chases and catching criminals! Nonetheless, I modestly say it became apparent to those above me that I carried qualities they were looking for with regards to leadership. Within just three years of service, I became a trainee detective and passed my Sergeant's exam.

The aspiration I carried from the outset was to be a detective and so I sought to get to the bottom of every crime I recorded; something most officers today would rarely consider doing, but this was a matter of personal pride to us twenty-eight years ago. My ardency meant that I'd be the one volunteering for the more complex and challenging shouts[12] put out over the air.[13] Then again, we didn't have the same volume of calls for service that we seem to have now. It was busy, but we managed a case from cradle to grave, unless it was really serious. In such an event we would do everything necessary before handing it to the CID (Criminal Investigation Department).

The first seven years in my policing career flew by. Starting out as a probationary officer in July 1994 at Stretford, it was August 1997, when I stepped into the role as trainee detective that my dream started to become a reality. In 1998-9, after six months as Temporary Sergeant at Stretford, I passed my promotion board and was promoted to Sergeant at Longsight, South Manchester. I initially served on Response[14] before undertaking six months as the Custody Sergeant, during which time I was successful in the selection process for the *Accelerated Promotion Course*, which was scheduled for the following year. As I received this news, the Force decided that I would benefit from some 'strategic development' and so I was seconded from operational policing to the Corporate Development Department,[15] which positioned me for the next twelve months in a team implementing ideas for improving efficiency and effectiveness in policing [aka the Best Value team].

In January 2001, I accepted the role of Detective Sergeant and was further promoted to Response Inspector for North Manchester in September 2001. Wow… seven years of exposure and experience of frontline operational policing roles in uniform and CID, alongside loving the opportunity to equip and support others in service delivery, I really couldn't have asked for anything more.

Outside of work, I continued to pursue fitness and competitive sport through my membership at David Lloyd Leisure,[16] playing hockey for Alderley Edge with former university friends, (shout out to Doody, Claire, Rachel, Nicky, Skippy, Sarah, and Jacqui) as well as representing Manchester City Ladies Football Club. Many fond memories of Saturday hockey and Sunday football!

In August 2002, I transferred to West Midlands police to become Sector Inspector in Handsworth, Birmingham. I loved this, as I had my own small police station at Holyhead Road with about fifty officers responsible for response and neighbourhood policing. I undertook this role for fourteen months before moving to become a Detective Inspector on the West Midlands' Major Incident Unit [MIU], where the focus on developing investigative and leadership skills as a detective resumed. This role enabled me to cut my teeth in learning how to lead homicide investigations and becoming accredited as a Senior Investigating Officer [SIO], all preparing me for promotion to Detective Chief Inspector in 2005 on an operational command unit [OCU], this time at Bloxwich, Walsall.

I had found the transition in transferring police forces quite difficult and cutting a long story short, I returned to Longsight, Greater Manchester in 2006 on a lateral transfer to become Operations Chief Inspector.[17] For the next twelve months, I was ushered into a baptism of fire with critical incident[18] management. Thrown in at the deep end, I found myself dealing with guns, gangs, murder and other serious marauding crimes, in an area often struggling with significant deprivation and hardship. It was during these times I witnessed some of the most challenging policing contexts, leaving little space for the softer side of community policing, and during a time that would be remembered as one of Manchester's most significant surges in gun crime. At this time, Manchester donned the ferocious reputation as "Gunchester" and spurred the inception of "Operation Xcalibre" – a multi-faceted policing approach, which resulted in significant reductions and importantly, the longer-term suppression of gun crime on the streets of South Manchester.

It was also during this season of my career that I sustained a broken leg and some serious knee injuries following a ski-ing accident in France. Shortly after the accident in January 2007, I developed a deep vein thrombosis in my left leg with a scan revealing that the clot was already at my groin and on the move towards my lungs! What was supposed to be a simple consultation resulted in overnight admission to hospital. My best friend Jenny, who had ferried me there in my brand-new car, so far not driven once by me, left the hospital in my new car without me!

I wish to give my hearty thanks to the brilliant surgeon at Nuffield Derby, Mr Guido Geutjens, for the immaculate job on my knee, performing two operations, and the incredible care I received at St Andrew's Police Treatment Centre in Harrogate, who, through their attention to detail, enabled me to make an amazing recovery. It is at this juncture I'd like to say this: If you are an officer reading this book and you have not already done so, consider signing up to one of the centres today. You can become a member by simply visiting the Police Treatment Centres' website,[19] details of which you will find at the back. For the modest cost of around £8 per month, you will be eligible for physio treatment or mental health support for the duration of your entire service, (even into retirement, too). Think of it as three cups of coffee a month. Alternatively, you can sign up to the West Midlands Police Benevolent fund[20] who offer a similar provision and facilities at St Michael's Lodge.

I returned to work after my absence in the Autumn of 2007 and began my dream job as an SIO (Senior Investigating Officer), working from Chadderton (a subdistrict of Oldham in Greater Manchester). I was placed under one of the best investigative leaders I know, retired

Detective Superintendent Keith Dillon. This was one of the most satisfying, yet probably emotionally and mentally challenging roles I would ever undertake, although at the time of course, I didn't see it like that at all… I thrived on the long hours, the fast pace, the intensity, the attention to detail, the determination to get justice for families and loved ones, and the focus that these investigations required.

However, what I didn't consider was the impact seeing so many dead bodies and attending umpteen post-mortems, would have on me. I had no idea how this would affect me psychologically, let alone my entire nervous system. I also didn't take into consideration the reality that on top of this, I was exposed to all manner of trauma [from the job] on a frequent basis, (as many police officers are). The impact of cumulative stress on our nervous systems cannot be underestimated, which is *before* considering the level of pressure from 24/7 shift patterns, the relentless pace of frontline roles and extended hours, all of which increase cortisol[21] to dangerous levels.

Research shows that the hormone cortisol is elevated for at least seventy-two hours after finishing night shifts. It has also yielded results to show that those who work routinely more than fifty-five hours per week, are 65% more likely to develop heart disease. Suffice to say here that policing puts an incredible amount of demand on the nervous system, which can manifest itself through heart problems and high blood pressure the longer we are exposed to continuously high levels of strain. Cancer, obesity and diabetes are all conditions that we will be more predisposed towards with irregular and extended working patterns, sleep deprivation or irregularity and poor nutrition habits.

With all this background painted, a trail of breadcrumbs leading to my extreme health crisis appears to have been found. However, at this point it has merely begun to emerge... I was still in the fast lane and the road to burnout was intensifying. Where was I going to end up?

3

My Return to West Midlands Police

In 2009, I returned to West Midlands Police Force. Whilst I had thoroughly enjoyed my time back in Greater Manchester, as an off shoot from my love for the city during university days, my family were far away living in the South East of England. This, together with my dad not doing very well from a health perspective, caused me to want to be a little nearer and so once again a move to the West Midlands beckoned.

For the first few months back in the Midlands, I worked on a project evaluating our approach to guns and gangs, (relating to the integrated working practices developed across departments in Greater Manchester, just prior to my leaving). Sadly, the West Midlands force decided they were not able to invest into a similar approach. However, soon after the Force did undergo significant change which came to fruition in April 2010 as it transitioned from twenty-one smaller policing bases to ten larger local policing units. At this point, I was posted to the newly formed Birmingham North Local Policing Unit. (This area consisted of what had previously been three smaller geographical areas.) The next few years would see me juggling a variety of roles, during which time I met Sam Ridding.

Sam was posted alongside me as a temporary Detective Chief Inspector (DCI). We became good friends and co-workers before she moved on to become a substantive DCI. In June 2012, I was posted alongside four others to become a member of the newly formed Force Incident Manager cadre (FIM), overseeing day to day operational business across the whole of the West Midlands Police Force. This was a unique role, which saw the five FIMs trained as tactical firearms commanders and equipped to command spontaneous and pre-planned firearms operations. As a FIM, we were also briefed to oversee all critical incidents, including the general spectra of threat, risk and harm across the force area. (All findings were reported to the Force Executive Team Gold Commander.[22]) The role of FIM required a 24/7, '2-2-2' shift-working pattern: two earlies, two lates and two nights, followed by four rest days, (which was initially challenging having not worked night shifts in the preceding decade).

Now that I had a position that afforded four rest days in between shifts, I decided to commence my level-two fitness instructor training ("Exercise to Music" qualification). As a side note, I thought my professional life would start out as a PE teacher, not a Police Officer, because of my passion for fitness (it's interesting how life pans out). Needless to say, I was thrilled to successfully complete the course, with an additional qualification in indoor cycling attained through Les Mills RPM.[23] (Shout-out to Julie Emerson Webster, one of the instructors at David Lloyd Leisure, who was a massive source of inspiration and encouragement to me in both my weight loss and instructor training journeys.)

Shortly after, I submitted a 'business interest' to work that enabled me to teach indoor cycling on a weekly basis at some of the local gyms, (David Lloyd, Branston Golf Club and DW Fitness Club). This was to become an important stress-relief activity for me, although I was to learn later, that smashing out 110% efforts every time was neither the best plan for losing weight, or for overall health.

May 2013 arrived and hungry to continue my upward career path, I applied for the West Midlands Police Superintendent promotion process. Finally, I was ready for a new leadership opportunity as a Superintendent. Vanessa provided helpful feedback on my application form and gave me confidence to get my focus and preparation right. Sam, too, was supportive as always and helped hugely.

Meanwhile I was very committed to my local church, from serving on the leadership team, to training and equipping days in the arenas of Christian prayer and the prophetic,[24] to leading local and international prayer assignments. It felt purposeful using my professional expertise in planning and strategy within the wider Church context. All this and more besides, meant there was never much time to stop and pause a while... In fact, the ever-increasing commitments seemed to invade every sphere of my life as I headed towards fifty, as did my relationship with alcohol. I was oblivious to the truth that I was accelerating towards a breaking point. The forties for a female are a time of much change as she heads towards menopause. I needed to understand and accept that I did not have the same capacity as I did in my thirties, or even my early forties. Instead, I lived in denial and didn't let myself off the hook with anything. The battery charge was on its last power bar most days, and although there was a moment of respite in 2018, by October 2020 the writing was well and truly on the wall.

I will conclude this chapter acknowledging that whilst a number of those close to me had, on more than one occasion, suggested that I was doing too much, I was unwilling to listen and admit that they were right. As a result, I continued to speed towards impending burnout. Suddenly, everything collided causing my life and all I knew to come tumbling down.

4

Wake Up and Smell the Coffee

It was Sunday, October 25th, 2020, and my last three to four years of service, when suddenly everything that had been suppressed over the past two decades came crashing to the fore like a tsunami. Hidden away for twenty-two years, that which had been building up in my subconscious swiftly cascaded over into my body, mind and emotions. The secret storm brewing inside had finally erupted…

John Sutherland, former Metropolitan Police Commander who was forced to take early retirement due to encountering similar experiences to those recounted in this book, wrote in a blog for Mental Health Awareness Week, "During the course of their working lives, police officers are likely to encounter serious trauma on 400-600 occasions." John states that statistic is in contrast to most "ordinary people" who, "during the course of their lifetimes, will encounter serious trauma on no more than three or four occasions."[25] Whilst marvelling on this, I was reminded of several "wake up and smell the coffee"[26] moments that took place just a few months prior to that Sunday afternoon in October; moments I would like to share with you.

The first came in May. I was participating in our weekly senior leadership team catch-up discussing the extensive scope of my portfolio, along with the requirements needed to deliver effectively. To say I was sensing the build-up of pressure with leading and managing such a broad work portfolio, is an understatement. My deputy, who normally held one aspect of the portfolio, had been off sick since the end of February and the team leader, who was overseer for the other, had been moved to a different role. I was feeling the absence of two Chief Inspectors to support me and so was desperately trying to delegate. However, much to my dismay, none of my colleagues were willing to yield – neither team members, nor their own shoulders to take on any aspects of the portfolio. I was on my own.

Suddenly, and without warning, I found myself breaking down into tears during the meeting. I rose from the table, unable to hold it together and left the room. Two female colleagues came out after me and supported me with reassuring words. *What was happening to me? I had never felt as though I couldn't cope before...* They suggested I make an appointment with the GP[27] and before the day was out, I had managed to give the surgery a call and secure a consultation for later that week.

After explaining my situation to the doctor, I was offered anti-depressants to keep me going. However, I wasn't struggling with depression... What I wanted was to be prescribed an alternative – not just what appears these days to be the default answer to a lot of things, which is to 'pop a pill'. So, I declined the offer and asked the doctor if he would refer me to a specialist menopause clinic for the symptoms I was experiencing. I was at a low ebb contending with the perimenopause, acute stress, and sleep deprivation, with all the accompanying issues these issues bring.

However, I still hadn't smelt the coffee that was trying to tell me to slow down…

The second moment came that same month, at the time when I began to experience discomfort and discolouration in my left calf. I called the GP again and managed to secure a telephone appointment. Due to lockdown rules during Covid-19, we were not permitted to enter the premises of doctor's surgeries. During my consultation on the phone, I was asked to take a picture of my leg and send it via email. I did so and a short time later, I received a call from the medical centre asking me to come down to the practice immediately. All the strictest health and safety precautions were in place and so when I entered the surgery to see the doctor, she was dressed in an outfit that was more akin to boarding a spaceship for intergalactic missions!

My leg was examined, but the diagnosis was unclear. The doctor called the hospital, and I was asked to report directly to the Deep Vein Thrombosis (DVT) clinic to undergo an ultrasound scan and have some blood tests. Fortunately, the diagnosis was just a superficial thrombophlebitis, (an inflammatory condition of the veins, caused by a blood clot located just below the surface of the skin) and thankfully, the nurse was confident that it would not develop into a deep vein clot. As a result, I was discharged from the hospital, told to rest up and to take anti-inflammatories for a few days. It was an opportune time for me to reflect and "wake up and smell the coffee," but that didn't happen.

July came and so did my third 'wake up moment'; the weekend that coincided with my 26th anniversary in policing (Saturday the 11th). With my leg better, I would go out for my usual bicycle excursion, (which was to ride a mile per year of service). It was a lovely ride; the weather was good; it wasn't too hot, and the Staffordshire countryside was a sight to behold. However, when I arrived home, I could feel a dull pain encroaching on my calf muscle again... It hadn't been there during my ride, but now I had stopped it felt sore. I considered that it might simply be another thrombophlebitis flare up (it didn't feel like a pulled or strained muscle), so I didn't take any immediate action with regards to my concerns and decided instead to see how it felt the next day.

The following morning my leg was no better, so I decided that Monday I would call the surgery. I did so and I was told to head to A&E. After a couple of hours of waiting I was called through to see the nurse, who took my blood pressure and heart rate readings, commenting that everything seemed to be fine on that front. My bloods were taken through to be tested and I was sent to have an ultrasound scan. The results came back to which the nurse responded,

"I'm sorry Maria…this time you have a DVT."

"How can it be that I was here only six weeks ago, with superficial clotting being told that there was no likelihood of a DVT, yet here I am now back in hospital being diagnosed *with* a DVT?" I queried to myself. What was occurring presently, were physical symptoms screaming out that there was an incursion against my nervous system. However, I wasn't to know this. Not yet anyway.

I consulted with the doctor and asked what kind of exercise I was permitted to do. I was told essentially to rest and if I had to do any form of exercise, for the time-being it should be limited to walking.

"Walking? How on earth is that going to help my mental health?" I exclaimed out loud as I left the clinic! Exercise was my lifeline! The only thing that kept my head in a positive space! Walking was simply not going to cut it…so I began to research the topic of 'cycling with a DVT'. (Honestly, I didn't want to accept the GP's advice and truthfully, I was losing confidence in their expertise.)

Eventually, I found a blog by a female athlete who had suffered a DVT yet had managed to come up with a safe plan to enable her to continue her training. I paid diligent attention to her method, applying her advice as I got back on my indoor bike. I had to be painstakingly careful with my heart rate in order not to cause the clot to move up towards my lungs, heart or brain (as this could kill me). It was a balance – literally – between my sanity and staying alive!

The fourth and final "wake up and smell the coffee moment" came about six weeks after the DVT. It was late August, and I was participating in an online meeting with my leg elevated (I did take some of my doctor's advice). I happened to glance down at my wrist to check the time, when I noticed my heart rate reading displayed on the face of my watch rising rapidly. Hmmm… I was sitting, inactive, and my heart rate was rising… What was going on? Normally when at rest, my pulse would be around fifty to fifty-five bpm, so to see it pass 110…120…130…all the way to 200 and remain there for several minutes, caused me to consider that the clot was on the move and heading for one of my three vital organs!

I messaged my line manager and told him that something was wrong, and I needed to get to hospital right away. Thankfully, I was able to get myself there, the hospital being just a couple of miles away. I arrived safely and checked in with reception. Without going into all the details of what happened that afternoon, (apart from being sent to the wrong triage area and the usual wait), I was eventually admitted. I underwent numerous tests including an ECG[28], blood analysis and a scan. The cardiologist came back with the results and told me I had acute symptoms of Supraventricular Tachycardia. I was to undergo a further forty-eight hours ECG testing in the first instance and told that I needed to avoid strenuous exercise, fizzy drinks and alcohol, concluding with my pet hate phrase – to "rest more".

A blood clot and now ECG issues… The pressure on my nervous system was continuing to build. By this time, another colleague had suggested to my line manager that I needed a referral to the occupational health team. I could feel the pressure mounting inside; I had to take seriously the accumulating anxiety and lack of emotional resilience that was causing emotional breakdowns to become regular events. However, with my 50th birthday less than a month away and a holiday to look forward to I kept thinking, "Come on Maria… You just need to hang on a few more weeks, then you'll have the break you need, and things will settle down."

Days passed and I'd heard nothing from the hospital regarding the ECG test I was meant to have. Thus far they'd given me a diagnosis with little advice other than what to eat, what to drink and what exercise *not* to do. They'd left me suspended, waiting for the phone to ring like a love-stricken teenager. Then, something happened that seemed to be a Godsend. One Friday morning, my anxiety level had risen to such an extent that I asked for the day off work. I took the opportunity to chase the hospital with regards to the ECG analysis I had been promised. The receptionist was very understanding and said, "Yes, you are in a queue; however, we do have availability this morning at 10:30 due to a cancellation, if that is any good for you?"

Hallelujah!! I made my way to the hospital, feeling a sense of relief that I was beginning to make some progress with medical help.

The anticipation I carried that my birthday celebration and subsequent holiday in Turkey[29] with my best friend, Jenny, would remedy my situation, were soon dashed… Yes, I spent a wonderful birthday with friends and yes, I spent seven beautiful days in one of Tui's finest Turkish resorts. But I was not myself… My anxiety levels continued to be high, so I was unable to make the most of the relaxation on offer, and I couldn't even concentrate enough to enjoy a good book! The thoughts of a birthday respite to short circuit the descent of my ill-health was something to aim for, but sadly it wasn't to be and soon after returning to work from annual leave, the emotional breakdowns began to occur once again.

My appointment with an occupational health advisor finally arrived. As we talked on the phone and I started to describe the turn of events from the Spring, I became overwhelmingly tearful. Cataloguing a list of physical and mental health scenarios, she responded by advising I reduce my hours in order to give myself some much-needed time out. I agreed and she implemented the action within my workplace. When I explained to colleagues that I had been placed on restricted duties, one of my peers approached me privately and said,

"Maria, you cannot do the duty rota when you're restricted. I will pick up your duty responsibilities."

Extremely grateful for the offer, I wanted to protest. Deep down though, I knew that he was right… I was feeling incapable, lacking confidence and now I felt as though I was letting others down as well. This was the moment… I had finally woken up and smelt the coffee.

It's a tough place to be when your head is just not in the game, when you feel on the edge and as though at any moment you are going to break down in tears. I tried to tell myself to snap out of it, but I was overrun by the dis-ease. I had seen other colleagues suffering in a similar way at various times throughout my career, never understanding how they reached that point. Well, I do now. Traditionally, policing had not provided a safe environment for shows of weakness or struggle of any kind, especially within the mental health arena; it was a tough and relentlessly demanding environment much of the time. Thankfully, attitudes have changed a lot and if I can play my part also by sharing my story, hopefully together we can help individuals in high-pressured and demanding jobs to be better prepared and equipped.

5

My Perfect Storm (Unpacked)

Sunday afternoon of October 25th, 2020, I found myself without a compass, a map, a system of navigation, skills, or any previous experience on how I was supposed to move forward. It was as if I had been dropped off in Outer Mongolia without a dictionary, an interpreter, or a roadmap. I experienced a spectrum of emotions ranging from anxiety and hopelessness to frustration, anger, disappointment and grief. Grief was by far a stronger contender amid the emotional whirlwind, for it seemed as though all I had held dear in terms of livelihood, career, purpose, and destiny had suddenly been taken away from me.

Like it or not, I was going to have to come to terms with the reality of the downsize in my capabilities. I had to let go of the job I loved so much and had given so passionately into. Within my story so far, I have dropped hints of the instigating factors that caused, what I have called, *My Perfect Storm*. In this chapter, I'd like to take the opportunity to go a little deeper into each one of those factors for those of you interested in learning more. First, however, I would like to make some valuable assertions about stress.

What Is Stress and Why Is It important?

Firstly, stress is an inevitable and important component for all of us. It is important for performance and productivity in every area of our lives. We are created to experience and manage certain levels of stress, and the right amount of pressure enables us to function at an optimum level. It is when stress tips out of balance, either too low or too high, that we encounter problems. It is described by Medicine Plus, part of the National Library of Medicine, as "a feeling of emotional or physical tension. It can come from any event or thought that makes you feel frustrated, angry, or nervous. Stress is your body's reaction to a challenge or demand. In short bursts, stress can be positive, such as when it helps you avoid danger or meet a deadline, but when stress lasts for a long time, it may harm your health."[30]

There are three main stress conditions. These are defined as acute stress (the classic fight-or-flight reaction in response to a perceived threat), episodic stress (when acute stress is experienced too frequently, more often by people who take on too much) and chronic stress, (insidious in nature, for not only does it disrupt nearly every system in the body, but the individual may even be unaware of its presence, therefore feel 'normal'.) Chronic stress can lead to all manner of physical and mental health manifestations including cancer, heart attack, stroke, violent outbursts and even suicide.

When I first saw the diagram you see below – the pressure performance curve[31] (also known as the stress curve) – it was such a profound "a-ha!" moment for me, causing me to look back over the previous twelve months through a more technicolour lens. It made me wonder, "Why are we not providing this information as part of health and wellbeing to new recruits? Why is the UK Police Force not ensuring that all organisational leaders are cognisant of this detail? Wouldn't this surely enable us to better manage the health and wellbeing of our workforce?"

Pressure Performance Curve

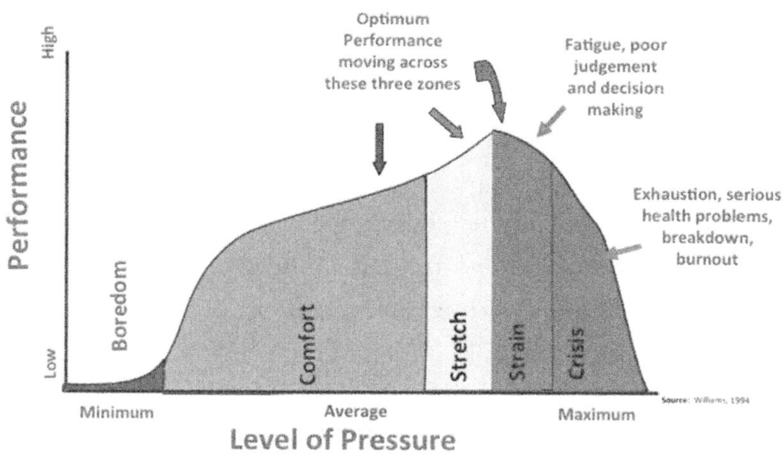

With this insight, we would certainly be more able to recognise the early signs of stress in co-workers and therefore be on a front footing, instead of waiting until the person has entered the debilitating arena of sickness.

Now we are armed with an understanding of stress, I would like to head into the breakdown of the individual components that turned the heat up on my nervous system, that is, the factors that led me to a point of being unable to cope.

1. Perimenopause (menopausal transition)

Although this subheading suggests relevance for females only, I would like to encourage men reading this book to gain a heads-up on what goes on with us women at this crucial stage of our lives. It really does affect everyone in our orbit and if men are more in-the-know, there will be better teamwork and support all-round. The menopausal transition will affect every single female at some point in their lives, meaning that at least 50% of the population will go through this phase of 'change' in which a female's reproductive organs wind-down to eventually stop functioning (the menopause). Some will transition into menopause easier than others. For many, it is an extremely difficult time, having a significant influence on a woman's ability to function in the way she has grown accustomed to. Because of its complexity, I have chosen to break it down into several subtopics before moving on to the next main subheading, which will be more akin for men.

One of the strongest characteristics that is generally applied to women, is our ability to multi-task and the self-confidence we can carry in our ability to do so. It engages our concentration, our focus, our energy levels, memory and recall skills, our emotional and mental resilience and critically, includes our ability to manage stress. We have managed it day in and day out over decades of adulthood. However, when perimenopause hormonal imbalance begins to affect us in our transition towards menopause, our ability to cope well naturally begins to diminish. For many, this creates fear, loss of confidence, anxiety, self-questioning and insecurity. I was definitely one of those. Not only do we experience many physical symptoms associated with estrogen and testosterone deficiency, but we also begin to experience an undermining of our mental, cognitive and emotional resilience. This is quite terrifying, especially if it has started without us having any real awareness or knowledge of what to expect, or of how to manage the symptoms and secure the best type of medical intervention. The issue is exacerbated by the very fact that so many GPs and other medical practitioners are not well trained or versed in treating patients who are transitioning through the menopause, let alone line managers and leaders in the workplace being equipped to support as supervisors. The lack of support and awareness means that, for many women, work becomes untenable. Research indicates that as a result, many women retire early or seek less demanding roles. Biochemically, the hormone levels at this point may affect a woman's ability to maintain an equilibrium in terms of optimal cortisol levels, leaving her feeling unable to manage stress in the way that she may have previously been able to and therefore, some adjustments need to be considered to ensure she continues to function at her very best.

It is important to note that whilst I am focusing on the menopause aspect, the cortisol factor is a relevant topic for everyone, because other conditions can cause this hormone to tip out of balance, which can be dangerous from a wellbeing perspective. The menopause is simply one context where the conditions are 'ripe' for problems in women.

The effects of excess cortisol in menopause

Cortisol is a hormone that is produced by our bodies and is essential to our health. It can be our best friend or worst nightmare through menopause and beyond, depending on the levels we have in our body. It helps by kick-starting us in the morning, physically motivating us with the energy to get out of bed. Our bodies normally produce cortisol in a cycle, giving us more when we wake, whilst releasing less near bedtime. As the sun goes down and the call for us to relax into slumber goes out, our cortisol levels should naturally decline and pass the baton onto melatonin, the hormone that induces sleep. However, as with stress, when cortisol levels become higher or lower than normal, and for prolonged periods, our wellbeing can be compromised.

What is cortisol and why does our body need it?

Cortisol is nick-named the 'stress hormone' and is one of the most important hormones within our body's endocrine system, making it essential to life. It holds three powerful and essential properties that keep us alive:

1. It increases blood sugar, therefore supporting the supply of energy
2. it stabilises blood pressure and
3. it neutralises inflammation (that is, our body's process of fighting against things that harm it).

Cortisol is a hormone within the 'major' division of the endocrine system and if deficient, it is important to get its balance restored. When under duress, our body releases two hormones, namely cortisol and adrenaline. Both are produced in the part of the endocrine system called the adrenal glands (these sit on top of our kidneys). **Both tend to work especially hard during menopause and when experiencing high stress.** They serve as our 'fight, flight or freeze' reactors. They give us sudden bursts of energy, focus, and increased alertness when something like a Sabre Tooth tiger leaps out of the bushes or, more realistically, when we experience extreme life changes!

Why does stress make menopause symptoms worse?

When highly stressed, our bodies maintain excessive levels of cortisol throughout the day. Over a period of months or years, heightened cortisol can cause serious problems across our finely tuned systems. Excessive cortisol can lead to adrenal fatigue (hypothalamic-pituitary-adrenal or HPA), whilst too little can induce a whole other set of challenges that could require a variety of therapies to resolve. The roller-coaster of a woman's endocrine system during her menopausal transition alters the way she emotionally responds to stress, often intensifying feelings of low-mood and anxiety, making it easy for her to feel overwhelmed and isolated. However, it is not only a woman's emotions that are impacted

– there can be repercussions on a physical level, too. Some of the most common initial reactions to excessive stress levels are a raised heart rate, changes in body temperature and changes in gut health. Other symptoms can include:

- Insomnia
- Low energy (even if getting adequate sleep)
- Frequent colds
- Cravings for unhealthy foods
- Digestion problems like bloating
- Weight gain (especially around the middle)
- Low sex drive
- More aches and pains
- Low mood

As mentioned earlier, if one heads into chronic stress much worse health conditions can arise.

2. Poor nutrition

Hormonal imbalance alongside poor choices and planning, can and will lead to poor nutrition, which impacts so many aspects of life:

- Brain health, focus, concentration and mood
- risk of obesity and diabetes
- uneven blood sugar levels with spikes and lows, causing fatigue and poor concentration
- an increasing risk of insulin resistance
- increased stress levels as a result of elevated cortisol levels and
- increased risk of heart disease, cancer and metabolic syndrome.[32]

Stress and nutrition are very much a two-way street in their relationship. It is no surprise that negative eating patterns arise, whether it be a reduced appetite or acting upon over-indulgent cravings. The wrong foods will create their own roller coaster of highs and lows, which long-term will impact sleep quality and overall health. If you would like to find out more about this specifically, I invite you to visit the website *https://nutrition.org/nutrition-and-stress-a-two-way-street/* in the first instance.

My typical response to stress from a dietary point of view, was to ingest too much processed food including refined carbs, sugar, bad fats and take-aways, which as a result meant that I had an insufficient intake of protein. This, coupled with not taking my designated breaks and eating irregularly at work, was a recipe for disaster. I would return home, usually having not eaten much throughout the day, and further graze on snacks (accompanied with wine) as the dinner cooked. And whilst many saw me as a fit individual because I exercised a lot, I had once again become obese, and this had happened fairly rapidly over the eighteen months leading up to my October crunch point. (As much as folk out there want to hope that it is possible, you simply cannot exercise your way out of a bad diet!)

3. Spinning too many plates

I had become overcommitted in every area of my life, inside and outside of work. Over-compensating in my desire to help others and doing things that were not required of me (I confess due to likely seeking the approval and endorsement of others at work), meant that ultimately, I was trying to mitigate feelings of low self-esteem and confidence, which were beginning to plague me. For example, at my local church I would take on far more than was asked or expected of me. I would gladly facilitate training weekends and organise group trips abroad, when I should've been resting. The gym was another area of contention; I should've just focused on my personal training, rather than teaching classes. Being over-committed in too many extra-curricular activities as I approached an age of critical transition, meant I was not getting the rest and crucial recovery time that I needed. The feelings of obligation, of not wanting to let others down, led to the next significant factor in *My Perfect Storm*.

4. People-pleasing and an inability to say "no"

Somehow, I had synonymised acceptance, endorsement and approval as a human being through trying to please everyone. I feared rejection from anyone if I simply used the two-letter word: No. Needless to say, this had a huge impact on my stress levels both physically (because I'd end up doing way too much) and emotionally (through anxiety).

It was when I listened to Dr Libby Weaver's book, *Rushing Woman's Syndrome*[33] that I really came to terms with this about myself and finally faced it. Incredibly challenging, her book enabled me to unpack the "why" and the "how" of what had caused my life to spiral out of control. It is simple enough to say that I had to undergo a real evaluation of my deepest motivations and come face-to-face with many insecurities. It felt very liberating, but I also knew that having uncovered some deep ingrained habits, it was going to take some time to re-wire my belief systems in order to live differently. I also knew that this would probably be quite painful...certainly at the outset. If I truly wanted lasting change and transformation, I knew this was the way and that it called for one-hundred percent commitment. (A learning curve that continues to this day.)

5. Poor sleep

This is the backbone that, upon reflection, is possibly the most fundamental to alleviating and lowering stress levels. Without quality sleep, (which I experienced for some time), cortisol levels will be undesirably elevated and overall, an imbalance of our entire endocrine system will occur. We will grow an appetite for unhealthy food, consumption of which we now know will further elevate stress levels, which in turn will reduce sleep quality and quantity…and so the cycle continues.

Having looked at other factors which can elevate stress during sleep, research indicates that unsurprisingly it can also be caused by external noise or interruptions, an inadequate mattress, insufficient exercise or fresh air, or by simply not paying attention to important 'sleep hygiene'[34] approaches. I have used a Garmin Fenix[35] watch since November 2019, a watch that measures heart rate and heart rate variability[36] (HRV) on a continual basis, which has been a great tool to provide feedback on my sleep and stress levels. Below, I have added the URL to an article by WHOOP health initiative providing a great explanation of HRV, detailing its significance when it comes to overall health. If you would like to read it, I invite you to visit https://www.whoop.com/en-gb/thelocker/heart-rate-variability-hrv/.

Purely from the interest of a bystander, I thought I'd show you what this fantastic watch I've been plugging looks like and while I'm at it, give you an idea of where my personal HRV and sleep levels were at just before that Sunday afternoon of 25th October 2020. For ease of interpretation, deep sleep should be between 13-23% of total sleep and REM sleep 20-25%. The optimal average stress level score for a day should be between 20-30 and in Garmin connect, you receive a warning message akin to "make sure you take time to rest and recover or you will become exhausted".

Screenshot 1, 8th January 2020

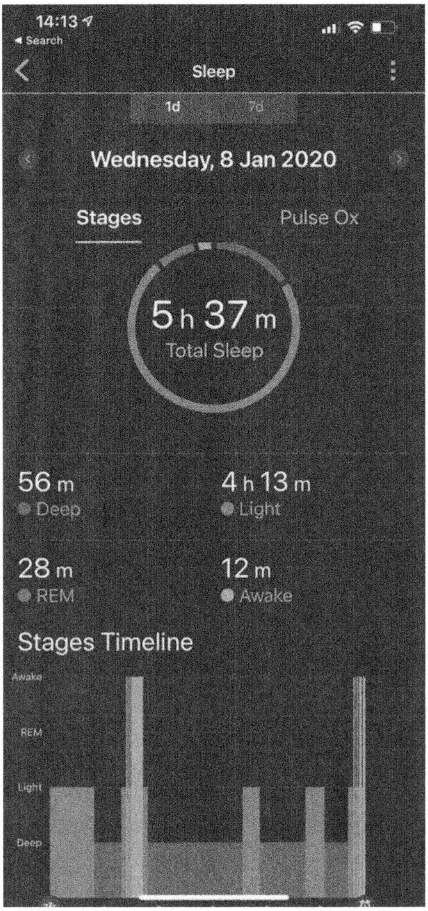

Sleep

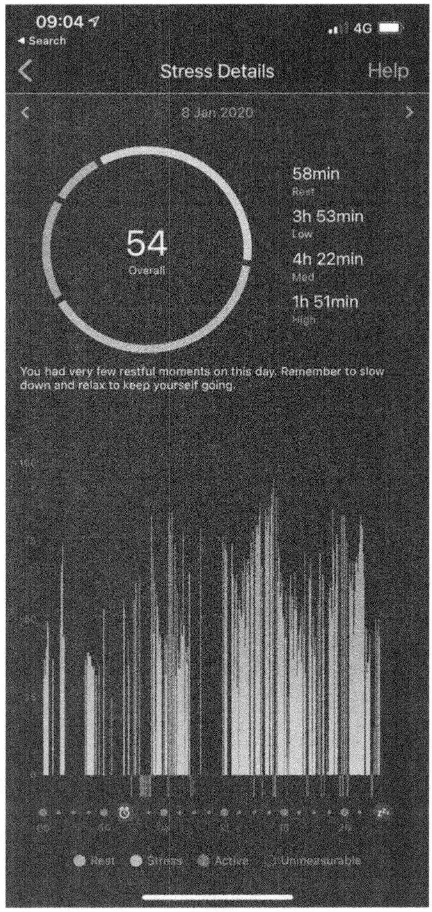

Stress

The screenshots illustrate sleep and stress datasets for the same time-period. What I find particularly significant is that on this day (and the previous), I had consumed half-a-bottle to a bottle of wine. This would have without doubt impacted my stress levels and sleep quality. The comparison screenshots you'll see later in this chapter, were at a time when no alcohol had been consumed for around forty days. I could share screenshot after screenshot that shows how significantly alcohol impacts stress levels and sleep quality, and how, in its absence, the body begins to rest and recover. I explore the alcohol factor a little deeper in a later chapter.

Experts say that optimal sleep should be between 7-9 hours and, looking at the above screenshots, there should be several periods of the dark blue band [for those reading in colour], signifying deep sleep (also called 'slow-wave'). According to Sleep Foundation, research indicates that deep slumber is important for "specific physical and mental benefits". Staff writer Danielle Pacheco goes on to explain, "During deep sleep, your body releases growth hormone and works to build and repair muscles, bones, and tissue, and immune system functioning. Additionally, slow-wave sleep may be important for regulating glucose metabolism."[37]

During sleep, we should also experience what's known as REM sleep (Rapid Eye Movement) which, according to Sleep Foundation "plays an important role in dreaming, memory, emotional processing, and healthy brain development."[38] Both deep and REM types of sleep are essential for our brain and body to rest and recover. For your interest, what follows are two screenshots of how a normal (or low) stress image should look during a 24-hour period, along with what quality sleep should look like (according to the Garmin Fenix watch). Both images are taken from the period approximately six to eight weeks after I had started my recovery journey in October of 2020, during which I was resting and sleeping a lot of the time! These are better viewed in colour so head over to my website for a closer look in the section on alcohol free living [www.livewellandfree.co.uk]

Screenshot 2, 5th December 2020

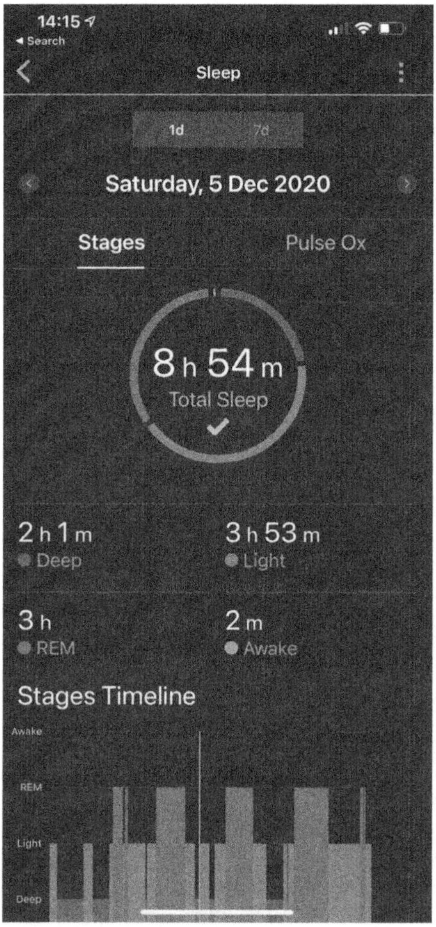

Sleep

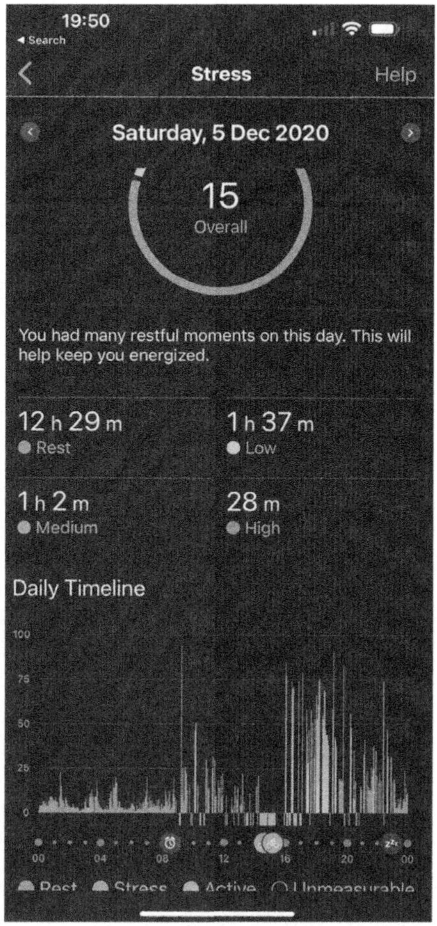

Stress

6. Minimal rest and downtime

Society (under the nuance of "progress") has fashioned us to become 24/7, "on demand" citizens. Taken from the Jewish Sabbath observance held each Saturday, the Christianisation of the Western World adopted Sunday to be the 'day of rest' – a day set aside to relax, replenish and be strengthened for the week ahead; a statute of the Judeo-Christian faith that our nation once strongly aligned itself to.[39] In the Creator's rhythm of life, the Bible tells us that a day of rest was fashioned into the weekly cycle. The famous Judeo-Christian patriarch, Moses, penned these words in Genesis 2:3, "God blessed the seventh day and separated it as holy; because on that day God rested from all his work which he had created, so that it itself could produce." (Complete Jewish Bible version [CJB].)

Although a Christian myself, keeping a rest day was something I had seemed to ignore for much of my life, probably through my relentless vigour for work, along with being swept forward by the ever-changing tide of our culture. The church that I belong to, began some time ago, to fully embrace our Judeo-Christian roots, choosing to observe the yearly, monthly, and weekly customs (as passed on to our Jewish forefathers by God), because of the life-giving qualities they impart. Ultimately, whether you are someone who shares my faith, or possess a different faith, or have none – the fact of the matter remains that we are not designed or wired to be on-the-go all of the time. It is simple science that tells us how, in order to stay healthy and function optimally, we must rest.

7. Excessive workload demand

This was another obvious factor that was increasingly encroaching upon my life, thus leading to higher stress levels. It was probably no more excessive for me than it had been at various times during my role as a senior leader in policing; however, entering my menopause transition at a time of increased workload, and a key leadership gap on my team, it was probably the straw that broke the camel's back.

8. Exercising too intensely (and too frequently)

This probably was one of the hardest things for me to accept in the early stages of my journey to recovery. In fact, I really didn't want to accept it at all! Now two years on, I can say that it has been one of the most liberating discoveries I made. Looking at the relationship I've had with exercise over the course of my life, most especially in the lead up to my breakdown, there were a lot of factors driving my obsession:

- I loved, and continue to love, the natural feel-good endorphin release and impact on my brain chemistry (very commendable)
- I liked, and still like, to be fit (very commendable)
- I enjoyed, and still enjoy, outdoor pursuits such as cycling, skiing and walking that weaves my path through beautiful countryside (very commendable)
- I was however, driven to smash every workout, thinking it would help reduce my ballooning size (not commendable)
- I believed my exercise intensity would prevent further weight gain (a myth) and
- I was driven to exercise to mitigate the guilt I felt around my alcohol consumption (not commendable).

Well, here we are back to the cortisol element! Every time we exercise, we produce it and as I have already described in the initial portion on stress, there is no problem with this – except when it is prolonged and sustained over frequent periods. For a peri-menopausal (even post-menopausal) woman, the impact can be extremely detrimental not only to overall stress levels, but also ironically *towards* obesity and weight gain!! I know some of you girls reading this right now are gasping, jaw-dropped and want to know more! Because fat is a slow-burn fuel, most people will only burn fat when they are exercising at lower intensity levels. (Good news for many!) What higher intensity exercise does, is elevate cortisol levels during and post-exercise for a longer period, so contrary to what you may have heard, the science (and my own battles with weight) stipulates that fat-burning is *inhibited until those levels reduce.*

It is also important to highlight that age, gender, genetic predisposition and individual hormone balance, will also be factors in our metabolism's choice of fuel. Although in the main carbohydrates are the fuel of choice for higher intensity efforts, fat *can* be broken down for fuel when we are exercising at lower intensities. Also, if the body is constantly in a stressed "fight or flight" state (as mine was), it cannot burn fat stores. So, in my case exercise may have given my mind temporary relief, but it was not giving my nervous system any comfort. It was simply turning up the heat and making things worse!

9. Increasing alcohol consumption (for any reason)

I have already made significant reference to this topic, referencing that I have a chapter dedicated to discussing its place in our lives. I have known such freedom since navigating to a place where alcohol is no longer associated with or defines any of the best parts of me. That has been a wonderful and phenomenal discovery!

The main point I want to make in this section is that whilst many are duped, as I certainly was, into believing society's message that alcohol helps us to unwind and de-stress, I have shown you evidence to the contrary by means of the Garmin screenshots. They are not only stark, but quite powerful in terms of demonstrating alcohol's real impact on our stress levels and nervous system.

Something else I have learnt along the way is that our liver, (the organ that eliminates toxins from our body), takes thirty days to reset after *any* amount of alcohol consumption. This means that our liver function is severely undermined when drinking alcohol on a regular basis. It therefore cannot function at optimal levels unless it has frequent breaks from the toxins that alcohol contains.

10. Little time for contemplation, prayer and reflection

Finally, as a Christian, my faith had always been a foundational aspect of how I understood my role in policing. I had joined from a very vocational perspective believing strongly that this was a "calling"; I was in policing to make a difference to the lives of those I led and the communities we served. Prayer and Christian meditation had both been aspects that I had cultivated well during most of my service in policing. However, in the latter years it had become lower on my list of priorities due to the increase of my fitness goals and work demands. In order to keep [my] equilibrium, if I could have got anywhere near to what German priest and composer Martin Luther said, I would have no doubt avoided my train crash:

> *"I am so busy now that if I did not spend three hours each day in prayer, I could not get through the day."*[40]

I may not manage to spend three hours in reflective prayer every day, but I understand what Martin is saying. It's the joy and restoration a believer experiences when in The Creator's presence and as such, I echo his sentiments.

As another very long-time policing friend, Sara Glen, and former DCC of Hampshire police said to me midway through my recovery journey, "Fox, the problem with you is that you are an adrenaline junkie and as you get older your nervous system just isn't built to cope with it all! It's no wonder you crashed!". She was right and thankfully, I know that this is not a subject that I will have to re-take.

Many people who find themselves where I was never fully recover and in policing, are often medically retired or pensioned out of their service prematurely. I want to bring a message of hope with my book that with the right approach and care, you can fully recover by taking control of the key health building-blocks.

6

Friends Looking from the outside In

Friends are important. Make sure you have at least two or three good ones…you never know – you may really need them one day. As for me, I can say they were a life-line through my difficult time. I find it amusing to speak now of the very small number of friends I allowed into my vulnerable space, for here was I, one of the biggest extraverts on the planet, not only needing, but *wanting* to go into hibernation. My condition caused me to completely withdraw, which was definitely made easier by the eruption of the pandemic that year.

It was the autumn of 2020 and lockdown measures had been put in place once again in our nation. The government allowed limited mixing indoors, which made withdrawing very simple! My indoor 'family bubble' consisted of my best friend Jenny, her husband Steve and Jenny's dad, John. Outside of these three, my emotional capacity was so limited I could only cope with a few additions to the 'family bubble':

- Buddy number 1 – Jenny, my best friend of thirty years. Jenny said she had never witnessed my being so withdrawn in all her time of knowing me (and that wasn't as a result of Covid).
- Buddy number 2 – Vanessa, whom I met during the 07/94 intake at Greater Manchester. Vanessa quipped how uncharacteristically uncommunicative I had become and began to really worry about me when instead of laughing at her jokes, I cried! (I wasn't crying because the jokes were so horrendous – honest!)
- Buddy number 3 – Sam. Formerly DCI of Birmingham North, but now Detective Superintendent with responsibility for all Homicide investigations and the Locate department within Force CID, WMP. Sam telephoned me pretty much every day to check in on me, (except Christmas Day when she texted me instead). Besides, she knew I was hanging out with my 'family bubble').
- Buddy number 4 – Jane, who had loyally tried to warn me of her concerns regarding the frequency of my alcohol consumption. Of those weeks and months leading up to my demise, Jane later told me that I wasn't the Maria she knew, sharing how painful it was for her to watch someone she had always known to be so positive and energetic wither into a listless, hopeless, demotivated, and exhausted individual, who could no longer seem to find her way in life.

These four friends were incredibly dependable and trustworthy. It will never be possible to quantify the unparalleled value of their friendship both before my breakdown and during the first six months, during which time the foundations for a full, and incredible recovery were built. They were like a ring of steel around me, each supporting me in specific ways, bringing their uniqueness, acceptance and friendship at a time when I very much needed their reassurance. Their support was consistent, unwavering, loyal, patient and encouraging. They always gave me hope that there was a light at the end of the tunnel and that light would appear nearer and nearer, in the weeks and months to come. And indeed, it did. They gave me space when I needed it and never pushed me into a position that might have added to my overwhelm or undermined my recovery, and always offered wise counsel, with firmness when needed.

Jenny and Steve were my next-door neighbours and I would often share meals with them. To my eyes this was God's provision, for it surely would've been a lot more challenging had they not been so close by. Despite my feelings of wanting to be alone most of the time, they were there if I needed them, which was such a security.

During the summer just prior, when freedoms had increased temporarily, Jenny and I had enthusiastically taken down the glass separation between our respective balconies. This meant that we enjoyed the luxury of accessing each other's houses via our level one lounges! What with Jenny and Steve next door, regular contact with Jane, daily phone calls from Sam (up to her eyes in homicide investigations, but still making time to check in with me as she headed home), topped and tailed by calls at the beginning and end of each week from Vanessa, (with text messages in between), I was covered.

My faith in God also underwent some testing times, especially in those early weeks before I began to re-gain some momentum. I knew God was there, but even my connection to Him was very difficult for I confess that probably to some degree I wanted someone to blame! As the weeks went by, my circle slowly widened to include a few other contacts from work who maintained regular contact with me: Kelly, Caz, Bello from my teams and Emma, (who had been appointed my welfare officer), also Sara, Jane, Marianne, Rod, Sarah and Matthew.

For those closest to me, at times they confessed to feeling as though they were treading on eggshells... The sad reality was, I was so emotionally fragile that the slightest thing would cause me to implode and have an emotional outburst. Everything felt so out of control...my emotions, the health challenges I was facing, my mindset and my mental resilience. This was all intensified by what was a lack of support from the medical profession, leaving me unable to get the answers and interventions that I needed. At least for now I did not have to worry about work, which meant I was able to begin to focus on the things that I *could* do...namely, recover.

7

Out of Control vs Taking Control

In the days and weeks that followed October 25th, 2020, I felt as though I was in completely uncharted waters. I had reached a point where I truly did not know how to move forward.

The debilitating short-term memory losses and becoming increasingly befuddled with tasks, would leave me emotionally wrecked. Now I am on hormone replacement therapy (HRT) and equipped with plenty of mitigating actions, thankfully these scenarios are fewer in frequency and less detrimental to my quality of life when they do occur.

My experience with the local GP surgery in the early weeks was less than helpful and particularly the inability to have any control over medical interventions, something which I know will resonate with many females in perimenopause. This ultimately led to me spending a significant amount of money to receive the correct treatment via a private specialist menopause and wellbeing practice, Newson Health.

Between May and October 2020, I had undergone seven consultations with various GPs from my surgery, ranging from consultations in relation to perimenopause symptoms, suspected thrombosis, and ECG issues. Whilst sympathetic, the GPs at the practice were simply not equipped with the sufficient expertise to deal with a patient who had a health background such as mine and who was crying out for HRT to support an ever-intensifying perimenopause.

I remember sitting at my kitchen table one dark November afternoon, crying during the video consultation with one of the GPs as I finally accepted that I would have to give anti-depressants a go. The doctor had provided many reasons why I could not be prescribed HRT (that were later found to be completely inaccurate; however, I won't expound on this now). In later correspondence and responding to a formal complaint I had made, the GP detailed further reasons why I wasn't eligible for the medication, including one relating to my mother who had according to his records passed away from breast cancer! Where he obtained this information from is beyond me, as my mother is still alive and well to this day!

Reluctantly, I made my way to the surgery to collect the anti-depressants only to discover that they were incompatible with the apixaban prescribed to me following the deep vein thrombosis! This was the moment I lost it with the GP surgery… I was fuming and, storming back into their pharmacy, threw the tablets on the counter exclaimed, "What do you think you are doing giving me these drugs when you know I am on apixaban?" The pharmacist offered the explanation, "The GP must have assessed the risk –" to which I interjected, "You can keep the anti-depressants!"

Reflecting on this episode more than two years later, I continue to hear story after story where GPs are prescribing anti-depressants as a "fix-all" for anything linked to a "depression-type" symptom when often there is a much healthier, non-prescription drug led approach, that can be embarked upon at the outset. In my case, I was suffering from burnout and acute perimenopausal stress; some of my symptoms may have looked like "depression" but I was not suffering from depression. I needed to rest; I needed a "reset"; I needed to regain hormone balance and I needed to re-balance brain chemistry; anti-depressants should not have been the protocol from the GP to address my circumstances.

To add insult to injury, the doctor had not mentioned any risks associated with what he had prescribed me, so the practice manager was now about to get it between the eyes! I progressed through a formal complaint process regarding my care, which resulted in an apology and an informal resolution with the GP. As a result, I was allocated a dedicated one-to-one doctor to oversee my recovery throughout the time I was off work.

In connection to my ECG results with Queens hospital, Burton-upon-Trent, I chased them for the report, only to discover that mine was stuck in a backlog, waiting to be reviewed and I was on a long waiting list. I was becoming impatient, and I wanted answers… All of this was only serving to increase my anxiety levels.

Notwithstanding the weighty sense of overwhelm and a feeling that the odds were stacked against me, I began to re-frame all my circumstances as an opportunity to be kind to myself; to begin a process of self-care that might help navigate me out of the maze I had found myself in. My new metabolic health gadget "*Lumen*" purchased shortly before that Sunday afternoon had arrived and was giving me a daily plan and approach to key health components. (See the chapter "Lumen Lights the Path".) I was now ready to go!

I have shared with you in chapter 5 the key elements that caused, what I have called, *My Perfect Storm*. In the rest of this chapter, I would like to recount to you the essential influencing factors that helped me regain control and return, step-by-step, to greater normality. I make no apologies for covering each one in some detail, because they may be a helpful signpost to either yourself or someone you know.

1. Counselling sessions

Have you ever had the experience of being somewhere in the dark, in an unfamiliar place, with no light readily available to illuminate your surroundings? I have too – most regularly at a campsite in the middle of the night! In a more surreal reality though, I had reached a place where inwardly I felt in utter darkness. To explain it another way; on a physical level I would go to sleep at nightfall, as is common for us all to do, but when morning came and the birds would start singing their dawn chorus, I was so tormented within, it was as if I couldn't see the light of day; the candle of my soul had become very dim.

Desperately seeking to understand and to somehow regain some normality, I made a list ahead of my first appointment with trained counsellor Henrietta; a list of all the things I needed to do to ensure that I could be back at work within two weeks.

"That should fix it all!" I thought. After all, I was known as 'Maria Fix It' to friends and family. Little did I know then of the long haul that was in front of me!

The thing is, my 'list' contained actions to address the *symptoms* that were manifesting, not the root causes; I was completely ignorant at this point of the notion of burnout, stress, and exhaustion, let alone it being an official diagnosis. The GP who had seen me before I was (gratefully) passed on to a more consistent and dedicated overseer, had given my condition the broad label 'acute perimenopausal stress'. I didn't want 'stress' as a label on my sickness record – surely that was seen as a sign of weakness and could be career limiting?

Thankfully, I was entirely wrong. I'd reached a juncture where my focus now was to try and take control of what I was comfortable with and able to take control of, which at this stage was the essential rudiments of life. This is where my sessions with Henrietta became invaluable. She could clearly perceive the mental challenges I was experiencing, so first and foremost wisely understood her role as a listening ear, offering tools, reassurance, and suggestions when the moments were right. She responded to my unique situation rather than some textbook guide on 'how to counsel someone with acute symptoms of stress and burnout'. This is important to emphasise because although there may be common threads and patterns distinguishable across the experiences of many, we are incredibly unique as individuals, and there cannot be a "one-size-fits-all" approach.

I would like to briefly expound on why these sessions were so important for helping me take back control. Firstly, I wanted more than anything to get back to work. Secondly, it became clear that Henrietta was the only person who seemed able to comprehend what I was experiencing; she listened intently and helped me to navigate steps forward in a way that met me where I was at. Thirdly, and most crucially to ensure a fruitful outcome, I chose to be transparent; I had nothing to hide and nothing to prove. By being open-hearted, negative belief systems hidden within my core were exposed, including anxieties and motivations of my heart, all of which required dismantling and replacing with truth. Throughout our discussions, reflections and musings, sometimes unbeknownst to me, navigational tools were being added to my 'survival belt'. Sometimes, it was by simply normalising some of what I had experienced so I felt less alone. Other times, Henrietta would affirm the point of discussion as "a passing moment in time," soon to be a welcomed, distant struggle.

Within her counselling strategy, Henrietta would use helpful visual analogies. My favourite was from within a 'horsey' context. I had learned to ride at six years old and my dad being a horse racing enthusiast meant I had seen many a race throughout my early years, (to the point that I wanted to become a jockey!). Paralleling my recovery journey to the likes of a horse's stable, its pasture, the paddock (where, as a racer, the horse would be saddled, mounted and paraded), to the starting gate, the aggravating false starts, all to consider the movement of the horse in and betwixt each station, resonated profoundly with me. She was simply brilliant and what started as weekly appointments, slowly moved to fortnightly, then eventually to monthly as she supported my transition to be ready to return to work.

A sincere statement Henrietta made near the outset of her sessions with me was how she could foresee me one day being an "expert" in all of this and in a position to help others. At the time, I thought how ridiculous! How could she see such a thing? And what kind of expert would I be, when I had got myself into this mess in the first place? But then again, isn't it one of life's pillars to take what we learn through hardship and turn it into something that others can benefit from?

Slowly but surely, I began taking back control of the rudiments in life; of what, when and how much I ate…of how much I slept…of my physical activity (being sure to monitor my stress levels and undertaking steps to lower them as necessary, which I share more about in a later chapter). Now I understand the 'whys', the 'hows' and the impact of those fundamental ABCs in life that influence so strongly one's physical and mental state. They are of utmost importance if we are to be the healthiest version of ourselves that we can be.

2. Sleep

According to Matthew Walker, British scientist and professor of neuroscience and psychology at the University of California, "Sleep is the single most effective thing we can do to reset our brain and body health each day."[41]

Sleep was critical to my repair and reset process. (And as we know, poor sleep increases stress levels meaning that those cortisol levels will sky-rocket!) Now if I find my sleep falls out of balance for whatever reason, I work hard to bring it back into equilibrium through the tactics and tools I have since learned.

In chapter 5, I referred to some of the main components that negatively affected my sleep (and will affect anyone's sleep): poor nutrition, alcohol, stress, and hormone imbalance. Having poor quality sleep sets in motion a domino effect on the rest of the body, with the next two hormones to be compromised being those associated with controlling appetite and satiation: leptin and ghrelin. And this is just the start... The bottom line is this equation: Sleep affects the brain chemistry and function of the endocrine system and brain chemistry, together with the endocrine system, affects sleep. Make good choices with eating, drinking and lifestyle and you are more likely to get the good sleep your body (and mind) needs.

With the alcohol factor now removed from my diet, within a week I was seeing a vast difference in my sleep quality. In a matter of a few days, I began to sleep longer and more deeply, up to nine, ten, eleven and even occasionally twelve hours! I obviously needed it... My body and brain had literally instigated a complete reset process. Four months down the line Sam, performing her regular check-in of me, commented that I might need to adjust this lest I never be able to get up for work when I returned! I chuckled as I assured her that my body would probably re-adjust once the main repair time was over.

Sure-enough, in months five and six, my sleep dropped down to a routine eight to nine hours (with the occasional ten hours). This sleep felt blissful – I just could not get enough! It was amazing to experience how my body was using this time to repair my physical and mental structures from the cumulative effect of diagnosed burnout and chronic fatigue; exhaustion that had built up over the months – perhaps even years. Now my whole system was going through not only a reboot, but a software and hardware update, too! So, it will come as no surprise to you when I say that my overall stress levels began to fall as well.

I loved using my Garmin Fenix 5X watch that showed me how the sleep-repair was impacting my physical system. My periods of deep sleep (for physical repair) and REM (for brain and cognitive function) were coming back into a good and healthy alignment. There were no alarms and no early morning commitments, (save that of my morning *Lumen* breath measurement to receive my daily nutrition plan), which meant I was able to sleep as long as I needed to, before starting my day. However, although my sleep became truly restorative in every sense, my emotional and mental resilience didn't return as quickly as I expected... The development of muscle memory as I adopted new habits was going to take time and effort. Another aspect of sleep's benefits I was unaware of up until now was the pivotal role it plays in weight loss. I have since learned, with pounds lost to prove it, that sleep is well known to help reinstate a healthy metabolism – an essential weight-loss element.

I am pleased to report that my sleep pattern is still consistent to this day (its range being between 7.5 hours to 9 hours). Through the discipline of going to bed between the recommended hours in order that my body, soul, and spirit receive the restoration they need, I can be sure to be my best during the day.

3. Nutrition

Lumen, (described in detail in the chapter "Lumen Lights the Path"), became my daily metabolic sat nav. Upon waking, it would soon be time to take my morning breath measurement so I could receive my nutrition plan; a plan that would be based on whether I burned fats, carbs, or a combination of both during the night. It was just what I needed in several ways, but significantly it provided me with some structure for my days in being off work. I had invested £300 with my *Lumen* device in the hope of finally hacking my metabolism and I was not about to have spent that kind of money to not use the device meaningfully. Little did I know that my decision to purchase *Lumen* was going to be a game changer – a lasting one at that – certainly when it came to fat loss, weight maintenance and developing an "on fire" metabolism! If someone had promised me that at the beginning of my recovery journey, I am not sure I would have been able to put a price on it.

I still at times ask myself the question, "How did I actually get in this state in the first place?" Was it simply a matter of poor time management as an 'adrenaline junkie' or was it laziness? It certainly wasn't my lack of ability to cook nutritious food, as I was competent and capable having grown up with a mum who loved to cook and a dad who was a chef in his early career. My family had been steeped in good wholesome nutritious meals from the get-go. Perhaps it was the lack of self-worth and esteem that had subtly crept into my life, deceitfully playing its menacing game…

My *Lumen* device arrived through the post, and I enthusiastically began to plan (and track) my nutrition. I drew tables in my notebook and penned all the good sources of protein, carbohydrate and fat sources that I liked, detailing how many grams of the macronutrient was contained in a 100g of each food and a regular portion of each food. I pinned these lists to my fridge, together with a picture of the most recent time I had been successful with weight loss. I now had a visible goal of the outcome I wanted to achieve, my gadget helpers (the Garmin watch, *Lumen* and My Fitness Pal (www.myfitnesspal.com) and, I had a visible check sheet to keep me on track.

The effectiveness of my new approach to self-care became readily visible at my cardiologist review appointment. He checked me over, discharged me back to my GP, writing in a letter dated March 2021, "Maria has completely reversed her SVT issue with her change in diet and lifestyle." This was later reported as a headline in the *Midlife Fitness Files* of the Daily Telegraph, in February 2022 and January 2023.[42]

RESULT!!

4. Activity levels

Thus far I've covered the benefits that counselling, sleep and good nutrition made to my recovery. In the chapter *My Perfect Storm*, I mentioned how the intense exercise I embarked on only served to increase my stress levels. How could this occur? Surely, I knew all there was to know as a qualified fitness instructor, didn't I? The problem was, I worked hard, played hard, drank hard and trained hard on every level to the point of exacerbation.

I remember Julie, my friend and colleague at David Lloyd Leisure saying to me,

"Maria, on the exercise front, you should stop doing long bike rides because you're stressing out your body all the time. I want to see no more than thirty or forty-five minutes *at the most* on your Stages indoor bike and limit long outdoor bike rides...better still, do none."

"What?!!!" I can remember exclaiming, asking her if this was forever.

Laughing, she replied, "No, don't be daft!

"It's to help your body reset, so it isn't stressed, and so that you can burn fat. Now, your body is holding onto fat *because* it is stressed."

I took Julie's advice and when weather permitted, substituted some of my outdoor rides for walks. I utilised this time to listen to the daily input from the Live Alcohol Experiment I had signed up to back in November, in order to gain momentum on my alcohol-free journey.

It was at about three months in on my new less intense exercise regime that I decided to introduce some strength training in the form of Les Mills Bodypump. I had all the kit from the instructor qualification I had attained back in 2016. By this stage of my rehab journey, I had gained knowledge about the hormone deficiencies caused by perimenopause, alongside how the ageing process naturally reduces muscle mass and so it seemed like a good time to embark on some more focused strength training. As such, I committed to my Les Mills training three times per week for about an hour at a time.

Encouragingly I was soon beginning to see results, which created a significant feel-good factor and within a couple of months, I looked forward to my body pump sessions – a structure I have kept to ever since. I am proud to see I look the leanest, strongest and most defined I ever have. "Positive emotion", also known as enjoyment, linked to any habit or routine in our lives, enables us to cement the activity or pursuit as a habit so that in time, it becomes effortless (i.e., second nature). If omitted, it would be something we missed, rather than something we must summon incredible will-power in order to complete.

Through the right balance of nutrition, exercise, sleep and stress management, of which *Lumen* and the great advice from Julie, my metabolism began to be transformed enabling me to lose weight.

5. The November 2020 Live Alcohol Experiment

I will cover this subject in more detail in a later chapter, but I mention it here simply with reference to how it helped me take back control. My increasing alcohol consumption was sabotaging my health from several angles. Using the support of coaching, community and content from the Live Alcohol Experiment, I was able to take an informed break from the substance, placing me back on a firm foundation and enabling me to effortlessly eliminate it as one of the toxic factors in my life. Because the 'penny had dropped' as the saying goes, I was confident there'd be no backsliding this time. When the *desire* to consume alcohol is gone, there is no temptation. There is no sense of missing out or deprivation and so therefore, nothing to influence [one] towards choosing to consume it.

6. Proactive stress management for spirit, mind and emotions

The transforming attitude of gratitude.

In the early stages of my rehabilitation, I was beset with self-pity. I knew a change of orientation and perspective were needed, so I set out to focus on God and the spiritual process in all of this. My starting point was to aim to journal at least one thing on most days that I was thankful for. After all, although it felt as though my life was in tatters, I could still walk, I was still breathing, I had not been diagnosed with three months to live and quite frankly, there were many others a lot worse off than me. God still loved me, my friends still loved me, my family still loved me. I had friends and I was being paid whilst off work. I had a house, a 'stages-solo' indoor bike, my road bikes, a hot tub…in fact, I was very blessed – in so many ways. Counting my blessings, I tried to develop more of an "attitude of gratitude".

There are so many holistic benefits to gratitude, validated by mainstream well-being experts and scientific researchers. I list just five of possibly many assets:

1. Grateful people are happier.
2. Grateful people sleep better.
3. Grateful people have better health and well-being.
4. Grateful people have better relationships.
5. Grateful people have more resilience.

Looking back, I know that gratitude was important in my overall process, and it certainly helped to re-ignite and reconnect me with God, which was important to me. My Christian faith had played a pivotal part in my life ever since my teenage years, enabling me to find strength mentally and emotionally, as well as spiritually. It was my faith that led me to the next phase of support towards my recovery.

Meditation and prayer

I was probably about two and a half months into my journey, the beginning of 2021, when I realised that all my usual justifications for not having much time for prayer and meditation were null and void. I now, quite simply, had ample time with no excuses and so I began to allow God into all the chaos.

There was much I perceived that I had failed in: My work, my friends, the state of my health… To some level I felt as though I had failed God as well, because I'd mismanaged so many things in my life and, viewing the horizon right now, it was possibly all too late…

I picked up a book that I had read very near the beginning of my journey as a Christian, when I was 16 years old, and which had taught me so much about prayer and the Christian spiritual disciplines. It was called *Celebration of Discipline*, by Richard Foster; a 'how-to' book I had come back to during many times in my life. I found the chapter that focused on meditation, amid my soul searching, to remind me once again of some of the key principles. Alongside this, I began to journal how I was feeling, what I was sensing and my thoughts about the process I was in, as well as visualising the building blocks I could see that would help navigate me into the future, whatever that future was going to look like.

During and after each prayer-meditation time I moved into, I checked my nervous system's response, (specifically my stress levels), via the heart rate variability feedback on my Garmin watch. As was expected, engaging in this practice really lowered my stress levels. (I wish to note that Christian prayer-meditation is different to yoga, mindfulness, and other mainstream meditation practices though all of these practices are known to lower and alleviate stress). This was another tool in my tool belt; a weapon in my armoury; an anchor in the storm; and was something I tried to implement especially near to bedtime to enhance my sleep quality.

Happiness chemicals

I did not understand at the time the full impact of the [above] measures I was taking to help bring healing. Just as the cumulative toxic factors had caused me to break, all the small and positive choices I was making were beginning to help restore my strength. Now I understand that I was working hard to reset my brain-balance by daily stimulating the following hormones that have a direct and positive impact on brain chemistry:

- **Dopamine – the reward chemical.** (E.g., eating food, achieving a goal, getting enough sleep, having a bath…)

My focus on nutrition and eating well – even experimenting with cake making – was something I had never had much time for previously. I was able to generate plenty of dopamine as I embarked on baking healthy cakes and homemade bread. Additionally, dopamine was released through the weight I was steadily losing, sleeping as much as I could and taking long soaks in my hot tub!

- **Oxytocin - the love hormone.** (E.g., socialising, physical touch, petting animals, helping others…)

  This one might have been more difficult during Covid especially as I lived alone and did not want to socialise! However, in January 2021, I became a mentor for the Live Alcohol Experiment hosted by This Naked Mind in a closed facebook community. This was to be the first of many that year. This saw me making friends and supporting others on their journey into an alcohol-free lifestyle. Additionally, there was the *Lumen* Facebook community where I was sharing insights and advice to newcomers on all I had learned, as by this time I had lost about 21lb and was moving steadily towards my goal.

- **Endorphins - the pain killer.** (E.g., exercising, laughing, listening to music…)

  Exercise was part of my daily routine, and I would frequently listen to music either during exercise, or when resting at home. I must admit however, that I did not laugh a lot during the early months of my exodus. The ongoing snags with my new house were a constant additional source of stress – and that was not a laughing matter!

- **Serotonin - the mood stabilizer**. (E.g., sun exposure, reflection and harmony, nature walks…)

> I walked in nature almost every day, even in the rain. I would contemplate creation by listening to the birds, or in a moment to sense the wind, rain and snow on my face when it came, finishing the day with my prayer-meditation in the evening.

Even though many of the symptoms I carried appeared to be affiliated with depression, I am pleased that I chose not to go down the route of anti-depressants. As a result, I have been able to share a journey to restoration and lasting change that avoided reliance on medication, which at the same time dealt with the root issues – which may be a prescription you, or someone you know, would prefer. This is not to in any way negate the reality that some will need medication to support their journey; it just wasn't the approach that I wanted to take.

7. Newson Health

In October 2020 I had signed up on the waiting list for an appointment at Newson Health, a specialist menopause clinic founded by Dr Louise Newson, created for women to receive unbiased and evidence-based advice and treatment, for their perimenopause and menopause transitions.

In December that same year, I finally received an email from the clinic to say that I could now make an appointment. My initial sense of relief was dashed however, when I was told the earliest appointment was in the following February. The prospect of having to wait another two months to be able to receive the right (and best type) of treatment for my acute perimenopause symptoms, was deflating to say the least. Nonetheless, I made the appointment for February.

With thanks to providence, it was only a matter of days before Newson Health called me to say that an appointment had become available for the following week, just before Christmas! I was overjoyed. I met with Dr Rebecca Lewis, one of the GPs from the clinic, who fully understood the turmoil I was in. She listened attentively and explored all possible symptoms, determining a protocol of transdermal oestrogen (oestrogel) and a progesterone tablet (utrogestan). She de-mystified the misunderstanding and misdiagnosis from my local GP, who had asserted from 2018 that I was ineligible for HRT because of my previous blood clot. A full hour was spent with me for this initial consultation, and it was worth every penny. I commend Newson Health to any peri or postmenopausal woman looking for answers and support, as well as investing in Dr Louise Newson's recently published book "The Definitive Guide to the Perimenopause and Menopause".

Finally…there was light at the end of the tunnel, with hope restored for relief of my perimenopause symptoms. The multiple medical referrals and appointments with specialists, from haematologist to gynaecologist, to expert menopause doctor and cardiologist, meant that pretty much every week I was having some kind of medical conversation to help me progress with my overall health. I still felt fairly low on mental and emotional fortitude - I still lacked some confidence, feared relapse and was very apprehensive about social interactions as they left me feeling exhausted. I soon realised this was not going to be a sprint, rather it would be a marathon…so I prepared myself for the long haul.

8

Lumen Lights the Path

"Embrace the long haul, for sustainable and long-term improved health outcomes!" This is now my strapline, over two years on from climbing out of my trench of dis-ease. Small decisions with significant results that over time, have produced the most incredible and dramatic all-in health transformation – physically, mentally and emotionally. I still carry the "wow factor" in it all to this day, for I continue to experience such a vast difference in my quality of life.

This, and the following chapter will focus on what for me, were the game-changers… The two main catalysts for my transformation, that of *Lumen* and living alcohol-free. I have broken this chapter up in to several subheadings for ease of your digestion (keeping with the food theme!).

The purpose and origin of *Lumen*

The mission of the creators of *Lumen* is to create a world, through the use of cutting-edge technology, where every person is empowered to improve their health through access to bespoke nutrition advice.

The vision began with twin sisters Michal and Merav Mor, two Ironman champions with PhDs in physiology. As scientists and athletes, they were passionate about developing a way to provide tailor-made nutrition for every kind of person. However, they knew the only existing way to measure metabolic rate, (which is the key), was costly and time consuming. After two years of intensive research and development, Michal and Merav created the first *Lumen* prototype, forging onwards to team up with entrepreneurs and tech-heads Daniel Tal-Mor, (Michal's husband and *Lumen*'s CEO), and businessman Dror Cedar, who went on to become co-founders.

Four years of hard teamwork and hundreds of beta-users later, the *Lumen* team launched on *Indiegogo* (a crowdfunding and product releasing site), breaking the £1 million threshold within weeks. Now, *Lumen* is leading the way in bringing personalised nutrition to the world.[43]

How I heard about *Lumen*

I was scanning through my Facebook notifications one day and an advert randomly appeared in my news feed. What really caught my eye and caused me to take a second look, was the name Chris Froome – four times *Tour de France* winner and my cycling hero! He was using *Lumen* to support his fitness performance and was featured advertising the device; there are now many other high-profile influencers, including leading medics, functional medicine practitioners, scientists and educators, as well as health and well-being celebrities promoting *Lumen*.

The advert explained how the device helps a person to "hack their metabolism" in order to know when their body is using fats or carbohydrates for fuel. I thought, *how incredible it must be to know what energy source your body is using*! Alongside fitness performance, the sales pitch indicated that this approach would help the individual to begin training their metabolism to be more efficient, enabling the loss of unhealthy fat stores whilst at the same time, becoming metabolically flexible.

Taking the plunge with *Lumen*

It all seemed too good to be true...but there was a full money back guarantee at the end of thirty days if you weren't satisfied in any way with the product. So, I decided to take the plunge. It was not an inexpensive purchase, coming in at £299, but who can put a price on turning their health around after struggling for so many years? (For me, it was from the age of fourteen when my yoyo-dieting began, embarking on just about every weight-loss scheme under the sun.)

I had absolutely no comprehension of the phenomenal impact this little handheld device was about to have on my life, with regards to my health, my professional success, my career beyond policing and my future. It wasn't until it came through the post, and I began to explore its functions, that it became clear this gadget was so much more... It was going to provide me with a daily guide to lifestyle choices that would radically turn my world around...

My favourite way of describing *Lumen* to others, is to call it a 'metabolic sat nav'. You might ask the question, "Why is a healthier metabolism so important?" It is important, because your metabolism is your body's engine. Much like when we add gasoline to a vehicle, food is the fuel we put into our engine (and why good nutrition is so important). As we apply pressure to the accelerator pedal and hear the revs and outputs of the engine, so this equates to our movement and activity. (Is all sounding good and working efficiently and as it should be?) Finally, with a good quality oil added to the engine, we should hear it purr...

Quality sleep and good stress management are the essential oils that keep our metabolism lubricated. The more efficient the engine becomes, the better the outputs. The healthier and more flexible our metabolism, the more likely we are to enjoy good sleep, good cellular health, longevity and proper immune function. We will also benefit by being a healthy weight, having improved fitness, increased energy and better concentration, with essentially, lower stress levels.

Lumen helps to inform our nutrition choices but also focuses on other lifestyle patterns. It provides a way of tracking our sleep, movement, fasting and stress management, indicating the impact all these things are having on our metabolism. Users often report within less than four weeks, how they are already feeling a lot better as a result of their bespoke daily nutrition plans.

What *Lumen* Looks Like and How It Works

Lumen is a small handheld portable pocket device that connects to an app, via Bluetooth on your phone. It measures your respiratory exchange rate,[44] (previously only something that could be undertaken in a sports' science lab or hospital context). The level of CO_2 in your breath correlates to your metabolism's choice of fuel. High CO_2 levels indicate your body is using carbs, (or mainly carbs) for fuel, whilst a lower CO_2 level indicates your body is using fats, (or burning fatty acids) for fuel.

You will recall me mentioning previously in this book about taking my morning 'breath measurement'. When you take a breath measurement, you receive a score between '1' and '5'. That score represents the following:

1 - Burning fat

2 - Burning mainly fat

3 - Burning a combination of fats and carbs

4 - Burning mainly carbs

5 - Burning carbs

When you take a breath measurement, you are aiming for a response of '1's and '2's in the morning and following low intensity exercise. You don't want to be consistently receiving '4's or '5's but you do want to see these numbers after you have eaten a meal containing a high level of carbohydrates (I will go into more detail later in the chapter.)

The *Lumen* interface also stores all your personal data and provides you with the opportunity to select one of three tracks: weight loss, fitness performance, or metabolic health. You can switch between tracks at any time by simply changing your goal in your personal settings. Again, I will explain how this works under the subheading *Lumen Tracks,* located further into this chapter. Essentially, there is a 'track' for everyone. I will take the opportunity to highlight now that it is not simply about weight loss... The overarching goal with *all* tracks, is metabolic health and surprising to many, it does not always correlate that slim people are metabolically healthy and overweight people are metabolically unhealthy!

Taking your breath measurement

Within the first couple of weeks of activating your *Lumen* device, it calibrates to your unique CO_2 range. In order to make this successful, it requires you to undertake breath measurements after you have eaten low-carb meals, then again after you have eaten medium-carb meals and finally, after you have consumed high-carb meals. This consistency is needed within the first two weeks. After this time, you can take as few or as many measurements you choose to each day.

The purpose of each measurement is to evaluate the impact of different stimuli. For example, after exercise and before sleep; when you are stressed and when you are relaxed; after a meal or at the end of fasting, when you wake...and so on. The two priority measurements in the programme are your 'morning' and your 'boost day' measurements, (to be explained shortly). Your 'morning' measurement determines your nutrition plan for the day, (essentially the ratios of protein, fats and carbs), whilst the 'boost day' measurement, (a high-carb day), is to measure how well you switch from burning fat to burning carbs. These two measurements are the primary way that the device captures a snapshot of your metabolic flexibility. ('Metabolic flexibility' is a person's ability to switch back and forth between fats and carbs for fuel, depending on the body's requirements and stimulus. Most significantly, it enables the ability to burn the optimal fuel in that moment for the body's requirements day or night.

A 'boost day'

A 'boost day' is a high carb day which some do perceive as a reward day. You receive a high carb [boost] day when your morning measurement reads '1's or '2's on four consecutive days (i.e., burning fat or burning mainly fat). On a 'boost day', your energy macros change from a *lower carb – higher fat* ratio, to a *higher carb – lower fat* ratio. This is to support your metabolism in its goal to become equally good at burning carbs for fuel, as it is at burning fat for fuel. The daily goal is to wake up in fat burn, because it is the best fuel for sleep (being a 'slow' energy fuel source) and thus will indicate that you have been burning fat whilst in slumber. Training your metabolism to burn fat whilst you sleep, will better support the maintenance of healthy weight as well as overall metabolic functioning and energy levels.

Your daily *Lumen* nutrition plan works using [what is known as] a principle of 'macronutrient manipulation'. This refers directly to a process whereby your energy macros, fats and carbs, change on a daily basis, dependent on your waking metabolic measurement. This enables you to navigate towards improved metabolic flexibility and efficient use of fats and carbs for energy, whilst ensuring you have sufficient protein to build and repair other cellular structures.

In a heartbeat

People within the *Lumen* Facebook community create posts stating that they are often surprised when they take a breath measurement and, ten or fifteen minutes later upon repeating the action, receive a totally different reading. To their minds, it raises the question of validity (until they understand how the metabolism works and it is simply the device responding to the requirements in that second). What might be affecting the reading at that moment in time could be any number of factors. Each time a measurement is taken, it provides a 'sit-rep' (to use police lingo) on the metabolism. As human beings, our autonomic nervous system dictates that we function in an unconscious manner, completely unaware of all the processes taking place to keep us alive and energised. For example, we do not consciously tell our heart to beat faster when we climb stairs; it automatically beats faster, because the muscles require more oxygen to complete the task. In a similar way, the metabolism is responding dynamically to all the stimuli our nervous system is dealing with *in any given moment*. Quite incredibly complex and amazing at the same time! We do not have conscious control of that, but we do have the opportunity to create the best environment for our metabolism with all the choices we make in life, giving reference to the 'Four Pillars' in the Introduction: Nutrition, Movement, Sleep and Stress Management.

Lumen 'Tracks'

The three 'tracks', mentioned in passing earlier, that *Lumen* affords a user to select from are: *Weight Loss*, *Fitness Performance* and *Metabolic Flexibility*.

Weight Loss

Should you choose to start your journey on this track, you commence by inputting your data into the app, (i.e., your height, weight, age, gender, goals, activity level, nutritional preferences [e.g., vegetarian, pescatarian or vegan] and any other specifics it asks for), then it will designate you a specific 'macro-nutrient' based nutrition plan. You can adjust your settings at any time if you think your overall allocations are too great or too little, or you think you should change your carb range for any reason.

Fitness Performance

This track has three separate goals built in to choose from:

1. Increase Muscle Mass
2. Improve Body Composition,
3. Improve Endurance.

For myself, once I reached my weight loss goal, I switched to the *Fitness Performance* track and selected the *Increase Muscle Mass* option. The most noticeable change I experienced with switching onto the *Fitness Performance* track, was consistently high energy levels, accompanied by good moods, encouraging levels of concentration, quality of sleep, a lower 'average' within my daily stress levels, alongside strength and cardio improvement, (i.e., a lot!!). I am proud to share that at the time of publishing this book, I am within the top 1% for my age and gender from a cardio perspective!

Metabolic Flexibility

If you do not need to lose weight and do not wish *Lumen* to design your plans around fitness performance, then *Metabolic Flexibility* is the 'track' selection for you. This track supports a sustained healthy weight whilst enabling increased metabolic health on a whole range of levels, (such as sleep, energy and mood). Additionally, the *Metabolic Flexibility* track helps your body become first class at fighting toxins, thus assisting the prevention of chronic ailments such as cancer, diabetes and cardiovascular diseases.

Notably, I have never felt 'hungry' since following the *Lumen* nutrition plans. This is due to the idea being about healthy eating *in response to your unique metabolism*. It is therefore a plan containing the accurate ratios of protein, fats and carbohydrates in order to meet your [energy] requirements; a plan which ultimately makes you feel fuller for longer, reduces cravings and helps you become efficient at using fats and carbs for fuel.

My feedback on *Lumen Feedback*

The *Lumen* gadget gives you great feedback: a situation report on your nervous system's current choice of fuel in real time. In each of those imperial moments, (even within a heartbeat), your body's engine chooses its type of fuel to burn (either carbs, mostly carbs, fats, mostly fats, or a combination of both).

What the gadget does NOT tell you is:

a. whether it is *dietary fat* that you have just eaten or *dietary carbs*;
b. whether it is *stored fat* or *stored carbs* being broken down (from storage in the liver or the muscles);
c. whether the body has made its own supply of carbs, (also known as gluconeogenesis – literally "neo" meaning "new", "genesis" referring to beginning and "gluco" referring to glucose]; in simple terms this happens when the body has a glucose energy requirement but carb stores in the liver [known as glycogen] and muscles have been depleted;
d. whether the body has broken down fatty acids and converted them to ketones[45] in the liver, to provide a suitable energy source

for the brain and muscles due to depletion of glucose stores in the liver and muscles.

All this said, one of the things I must not fail to mention is that behind the *Lumen* app interface there is a team of nutritionists waiting to respond to any questions and help that you might need. They do not operate through call centres – it is all automated through the app and is incredibly efficient. The 'robot' answers the most frequently asked questions, but there are real people on hand to directly answer personal questions and requests that the bot cannot.

My *Lumen* Journey

What *Lumen* offered me, was an innovative approach to the complexities of my health crisis and so having nothing to lose, (save ever-increasing excess fat!), I started my journey. Just when I needed a structure in my life and support for my health moving forwards, I now had my new gadget-friend to help me navigate – and it wasn't about to disappoint!

Not unexpectantly, the first number of weeks saw my morning breath measurements coming in at '3's, '4's and '5's. Despite this, I was beginning to feel physically better, experience less cravings, feel increasingly energized and attaining better sleep, as a result of my new discipline.

In month two and much to my encouragement, my weight loss began to steadily increase. I began to see a shift in my 'morning' measurements with my first set of four consecutive morning '2's being achieved! There were celebrations as I lay claim to my first 'boost day'!

Things continued to move on an upward trajectory as weeks eight, nine and ten saw a flurry of consecutive '1's. It felt like I had arrived!!

Over the entire Christmas period, I was on a roll and by January 1st, 2021, I had lost a significant amount of weight. There was a long way to go, but with HRT having now come onboard, I was optimistic that more balanced hormone levels would also begin to help. (Many people obsess about calories in and calories out, but research indicates that hormonal imbalances, caused particularly by stress, cortisol and insulin resistance, are stronger influencing factors when it comes to gaining or losing fat. If you'd like to know more, see **Myths about fat-loss** in *Appendix 1*.)

Gratefully, by May 2021, I had signs of my mental and emotional resilience beginning to return. I was regaining confidence and experiencing more consistent energy levels, along with an increased ability to concentrate and maintain focus. All this motivated me and boded well for my return to work. However, I was not going to rush anything… I knew and could feel that I was still in a recovery process and had not reached 100% yet.

For over two years, *Lumen* has been instrumental in helping me gain a lifestyle rhythm when to eat, sleep, exercise and manage stress intelligently is now effortlessly achieved. I still use my device to keep me on track and it is without doubt, a 'virtual friend' for life. I cannot see myself being without it, just like I wouldn't really want to train without my heart rate monitor, or my Garmin watch.

It gives me a daily protocol that I can follow if I choose; it helps me stay focused on the important things that my body needs (in real time), so I can remain functionally optimal. *Lumen* has proven itself through its results, giving me a recipe to become stronger and healthier day by day – in mind and in body. It provides early warning signs if my metabolism is struggling, therefore causing me to consider my activities and to adjust accordingly. It provides a 'sit rep' on what is going on in my metabolism and nervous system, nudging me to take care of myself in order to be better at leading and taking care of others.

I could take you through my entire journey…the highs, the lows and all the in-betweens. But I will save that as the subject matter for my sequel

– the focus of which is the story of my *50lb weight loss in seven months, sustained weight maintenance beyond twelve months*, with giveaways on *how to maintain soaring levels of metabolic flexibility*.

In the interim, I have created several videos documenting my journey, including a short video for *Lumen* asking me to describe the impact their invention has had on my health. You can find these videos under the heading *Lumen and wellbeing videos,* on my YouTube account: https://www.youtube.com/c/MariaFoxWellness. Please take a look and subscribe, as I will continue making more videos in the months and years to come!

I'd like to wrap up this chapter by sharing specific achievements that have turned my life around as a direct result of using *Lumen*. It has helped me to

- reverse Supraventricular Tachycardia (SVT) that initially was diagnosed as requiring intervention
- lose 50lb in 7 months – reducing me from a size 18 to a size 10
- reach a BMI of 22.5 from 30.5
- reach the top 1% for VO2 Max[46] in terms of cardiorespiratory fitness
- increase muscle mass and tone
- reduce my average daily stress levels and
- reinstate good quality and lengthy sleep into my life.

I am very pleased to have teamed up with *Lumen* to offer you a 15% discount off the subscription of their product. If you are interested in giving *Lumen* a go, I invite you to visit my website www.livewellandfree.co.uk, where you can pick up my affiliate link or you can go directly to the lumen website and use the code FOX.

9

Alcohol - Friend or Foe?

I named this chapter *Alcohol – Friend or Foe*, because in some ways all who consume it have a level of 'relationship' with the substance, whether occasional, regular, frequent or binge-drinking. I thought alcohol was my friend for many years, until I had the revelation of what it was doing to my life; that it was stealing from me and lying to me… I was finally beginning to wake up to the stark reality.

Somehow, the truth about alcohol had passed me by, despite one of my dearest and longest friends often saying to me, "It's not a health drink Maria!" as I supped yet another bottle of Prosecco or champagne on the beach...

Wasn't it? But it was oh-so refreshing in the sun, a justified reward after a long bike ride; the perfect companion to spend all day with me on the beach chillaxing… Or in the hot tub… Or on the slopes (or après ski)… Or by the pool… Watching TV… Or simply to alleviate stress after a long day.

Was my ignorance of its potential impact on my brain and body a result of being sucked into societal conditioning that says it's OK to do this (all in moderation, of course) and so therefore rings out as the epitome of some legal high? Had my steadily increasing tolerance level masked the reality that I was, slowly but surely, conditioning myself of its necessity for survival? It was a slippery slope that I didn't even know I'd stepped on until it was almost too late… No-one is exempt from the influence and power alcohol has – alcohol is addictive, period. It's designed to be that way and as such, with the right level of exposure and frequency, the brain will slowly begin to learn that it likes it, wants it…and *needs* it.

Giving up alcohol: Round 1

Before I describe the moments when I faced the music on my relationship with alcohol, I wish to re-wind to ten years ago…

I was posted to a role in policing that required me to work routine night shifts. It was a dynamic operational role, overseeing 24/7 policing operations in the hustle and bustle of the West Midlands. I really struggled to sleep after being out all night, especially with it being a decade since I was last assigned. So, I began to have a glass of wine to help me unwind and get off to sleep when I arrived home from work in the morning. (This, I believe, was the suspected moment where my descent into excessive alcohol consumption possibly began. However, although I was beginning to realise there was an issue, I didn't want to admit it – to myself, to God, or to my friends.)

About fifteen months later, I was posted to a new role where my hours switched to [mainly] daytime, so my drinking returned to evenings and weekends. There was always a bit of a battle when it came to alcohol, because I knew consuming it inhibited my sports performance, which I loved passionately (and still do).

"I will compromise," I thought "and just have a little..." though it rarely ended up "being a little" but my exercise levels remained pretty consistent, cleverly masking my dependency (and other rising mental and emotional conditions) through the natural high it produced.

Suddenly, in January 2018, my endorphin kicks came to a halt when I was knocked off my bike, resulting in my being laid up for several weeks. The writing was on the wall… With my mental instability slowly creeping up the Richter magnitude scale, my decline in health began to accelerate rapidly. The GP and others thought that the symptoms were typical of a perimenopausal woman and put me on some medication to boost my serotonin. I had not disclosed any details of my drinking habits at this point and so, still acknowledging it as my trusted friend, I continued to drink. Injured and now off from work, I could – and would – drink anytime, from morning 'til night. Yet…in the early hours of the morning, I would hear a small voice inside crying out, *"Foe! Foe! Alcohol is your foe!"*

I knew this to be the truth, but what was I to do? I could not contemplate life without it! I had done many an internet search reading up on what determines problem drinking, finding many a symptom checker… Now it was dawning on me that I was drinking because I didn't know how *not* to! My best friend, Jenny and others started to recognise that I was not well. Jenny for one had told me that she noticed me becoming increasingly agitated and irritable but was putting it down to the trauma of the accident and other hormonal challenges.

I avoided disclosure and when a moment afforded the opportunity to go skiing at short notice with my sister and her family, I seized the opportunity. I knew the mountains, fresh air and exercise would help my mental state and perhaps I'd be OK when I got back? Maybe I'd have nothing to admit, because the whole alcohol thing would be back under control...

During that week, I began to ponder on my lifestyle and face the truth: alcohol was the MAIN contributor to all my negative issues. Period. It was alcohol that was affecting my mental state. It was alcohol behind my sleep deprivation; and it was alcohol causing my soul torment, heightening anxiety and feeding depression. To top it off, my sister's comment over lunch one day struck right through the heart of the now crumbling tower of self-deception.

"You're becoming a right 'wino'," she said in jest.

"No, I'm not –" as I went on to justify myself.

Boom... She had hit the target, sending the tower cascading to the ground. I knew there and then that I had to learn to live my life without alcohol lest I continue the road to self-destruction. No more living a lie.

I returned home from our ski trip and came clean with my friend Jane. I told her I had finally accepted I was a problem drinker and needed to sort myself out. I was an emotional wreck and confessed I couldn't face anything without drink... But I had made the decision not to turn to the bottle again. Our 'friendship' was over!

✣ ✣ ✣

The next seventy-two hours were horrendous. I called Jenny and she suggested I make an appointment to see the doctor. I managed to secure one that same day and with Jenny there to support me, I outlined the range of symptoms I was experiencing, as well as my increasing level of alcohol consumption. The doctor asked probing questions about how much alcohol I was expending. However, this time, instead of glossing over the reality (as I suspect many patients do), I made a full and frank confession of where I was at.

His eyes opened wide when I told him how much. Speaking earnestly, he said, "I am really glad you have come to see me – and I am really glad you have told me. Now we need to make a plan to help you to stop."

"That's good," I replied, "but there's no need, because I've already stopped!"

"You stopped? – You just stopped? You haven't had a drink since Sunday?"

"No," I responded, "I've managed to go four days without one."

He started to express concerns about the dangers of going from all-to-nothing, but thus far – apart from being a little shaky the Monday morning – I hadn't suffered any other physical withdrawal symptoms during the week, which surprised him. I told him I had even done an intense indoor cycle class within thirty-six hours of my last drink! He emanated reassurance at my report, going on to brief me by saying, "Well, you need to have thirty days alcohol-free – if you can – and then I want you to have some blood tests to check your liver and general health. I'd then like you to come back and see me when you return from your holiday."

During this time, I found out that a friend and fellow instructor from David Lloyd Leisure had herself been on a tee-total journey for a while, so I connected with her on whatsapp. She passed on some tasty non-alcoholic brands for me to try and recommended two books: *Alcohol Explained* by William Porter and *This Naked Mind* by Annie Grace (as mentioned in an earlier chapter), both of which I devoured over the next few days.

I managed to get through the first thirty days successfully without a drink, but then just as I was entering month three, I had a blip – what we call in the TNM community, a "data point". Unfortunately, in my case I had clocked up a few. What I had done was to experiment with re-introducing wine into my weekends. *Why had I done this?* I asked myself, *when I had experienced such a euphoric sense of release the last thirty days without it.* It was clear that I was not as free as I thought... I was still a fish caught in its net. I was not as loosed from the grip of alcohol as I had led the doctor – or myself – to believe.

It became apparent that there were fragments of my thoughts and beliefs that still needed to be unpicked. I needed some extra help to give me a stronger footing, so I signed up for the new three-month *TNM Intensive* programme. It cost in the region of £500, including coaching, daily video materials to watch, journalling exercises, a workbook, coaching calls and a closed Facebook community (probably not far off what I would have spent over the course of three months on wine, champagne and sherry!). This was an investment for my long-term health and would also save me a ton of money in the long run.

I interject my story for a moment to share about the TNM approach. What I love, is the underpinning principle that – now this may come as a shock – there is no pressure to stop drinking. In fact, the approach is very much *stop* trying to stop and rather press 'pause' instead. Dig deep and don't stop digging until you know *why* you drink. Then, dare to face and begin to unpick those thoughts and beliefs, with the ultimate goal of being free from the *desire* to drink. When the desire is gone, alcohol is no longer a temptation. Its stronghold is broken.

I have had the privilege to write a blog for *This Naked Mind Institute (TNMI)*, giving my account. I wrote it under the pseudonym 'Louise', because I didn't want anyone in policing reading it and tracing it back to me! I felt so ashamed of the depths I had plummeted to and the potential stigma with such a story. However, now as a newly certified and accredited coach with *TNMI,* I recognise that actually, my story is powerful for creating a safe space for the conversation within policing, within public services, within the workplace; in fact, in just about any sector of life! There is no shame, rather courage, accompanied by a deep sense of motivation to help others in both prevention and in finding a way out. If you'd like to read my story in full, then I invite you to head along to: *https://thisnakedmind.com/life-without-alcohol-louises-naked-life/.*

It's important to understand the process of detoxing and if you are embarking, or about to embark on the voyage, to be kind to yourself. You see, the combination of our brain's ability to create muscle memory, together with the addictive nature of alcohol, makes it different to every other habit we form, because an addictive substance is involved. That substance is artificially stimulating the 'pleasure path' in the brain, causing the brain to release quite the opposite sensation: a depressant hormone. It is this that causes us to reach for the next drink, because the "buzz" we get from the initial drink is so short lived. Blood alcohol content rises but falls back fairly quickly thus necessitating the next hit. The more we drink, the more our brain prepares for the hit and the faster the depressant hormone is released, so that eventually, we need more, both to get the 'hit' and more again to retain it! (Phew! What a mouthful!) It's a vicious cycle of being sucked into a place where none of us really want to be in our heart of hearts.

I have included in *Appendix 2* some detail on the impact of alcohol on the brain and body, but I encourage you to read *This Naked Mind by Annie Grace, Alcohol Explained* by William Porter and *Alcohol Lied To Me* by Craig Beck, should you want a more comprehensive expose on the subject.

✣ ✣ ✣

I had enrolled on the *TNM Intensive* programme and I completed it, enjoying eight months totally alcohol free. Incredibly, from around month three I had pushed through the crave-barrier: I neither missed it or desired it! Across the whole spectrum of life, I felt a lot better, despite still struggling with some perimenopause symptoms, which I guess weren't going to disappear overnight (another long-haul).

In July 2019, I moved into counter terrorism policing as a development opportunity to broaden my partnership working and to further deepen my policing experience. At this stage, I had stepped off the tee-total wagon and had reintroduced drinking-in-moderation, though continuing to monitor my consumption and take regular breaks. I was still very conscious that when I did drink, it was always hard to keep it to a glass or two, and more often than not, it would end up being a bottle. *But at least it wasn't 'a bottle or two'*, I thought – or more even, I thought, as I compared myself to 2018. I was still keenly aware of its addictive nature and at some level had acute cognitive dissonance. By now, with all I'd been through, I knew the truth about alcohol...so why was I still pursuing it (albeit to a lesser level), when I had been so happy without it?

The truth was, I still had not fully unpicked some of the deeper issues connected to why I turned to it in the first place. My brain still connected it to both the need to alleviate stress and also to fill an emotional void – something linked to my self-value and worth. Alcohol was my friend at times – which feels weird to write – it definitely filled a gap when I was on my own and bored. I also continued to see it as a 'reward'; after a long bike ride, I would sit back in my hot tub and glug through a bottle of Prosecco like it was squash!

Giving up alcohol: Round 2

As 2020 progressed, some factors began to play out at work in a similar way to 2017, the year my drinking habit had first reached its pinnacle. I knew that both the quantity and frequency of my drinking was beginning to rise again… I needed to call time imminently.

Thankfully, with the foundation laid from the *TNM Intensive* programme I completed two years previously, this time around it was a lot easier. Additionally, and most importantly, I made myself accountable to my colleague friends Vanessa, Sam and also Jane, who kept a close eye on me. (I also did this during 'Round 1'.) There was no escape from being asked "the question" on a fairly regular basis and I knew if I tried to hide the truth, their policing skills would have found me out! Conversations would go along the lines of:

"So… How many last night?"

"One," I would reply, to which they would text me a follow up message saying,

"Glass or bottle?"

Slightly amusing to look back on now, but on a serious note, this accountability definitely helped me to gain momentum and remain on the straight and narrow. I recommend it as a valued structure to have in place and advise anyone reading, who may be in a similar place to where I was, to embrace it.

Finally, by the end of November 2020 I had managed to pinpoint, address and resolve the deeper issues linked to my stress, which began to have an immediate impact on my alcohol intake. I had escaped the entanglement of the net I was caught in and was swimming, wonderfully free, in the wide blue ocean once again.

December 31st came and I opened a bottle of fizz that my brother and sister-in-law had given me for my birthday, (one of his award winning 'fizzes' from "*Foxes Fizz*" at Sussex Vineyards). Sharing it with Jenny and Steve ahead of midnight to celebrate in the New Year, I hoped and prayed that 2021 was going to be better than 2020 had been. I had two glasses: no more, no less. That was it. My final toast goodbye to 2020 with alcoholic fizz. I woke with no desire the next day and with no looking back... Just simply gratitude that I knew I didn't need alcohol anymore. I had graduated with distinction and so now it was time to retire and place my glass back on the shelf...gracefully. Having now joined the team of mentors for the *Live Alcohol Experiment*, 2021 was a year of socialising and doing all the things I loved in life without the need for booze.

In conclusion

When it came to alcohol, I realised I had been duped by the lies of marketing, culture and society. I went from someone who reluctantly gave in to the peer pressure of drinking copious amounts of wine, to someone who probably encouraged others to do the same! I was the party organiser where the Prosecco was concerned!

When the balance tipped and I recognised that *it* was controlling *me*, the feelings of fear and entrapment began to invade, and I felt powerless to escape. The pretence, the justifications, the secrecy and the secret drinking all took their toll. Trying to hide the truth from my friends about how bad it had become and disposing empty bottles at the supermarket bins to cover up my tracks, all fueled the lie I was living.

I knew that alcohol had never really been my 'friend'... I was assuredly better off without it in my friendship circle. All I noted was that it gave me a short-term buzz, which added nothing to the moment when I took it, or to the people I was with. It didn't add anything of companionship to my life when I was on my own except misery, low mood, and nightly sleep interruptions filled with dread and anxiety. Alcohol... Friend or Foe? Definitely a foe!

If you would like to take a deeper look at your drinking habits or are at a place where you feel ready to take an informed and empowered break from alcohol, then I highly recommend Annie Grace's book, "*The Alcohol Experiment: A 30 days Alcohol-Free Challenge.*" Alternatively, head to the app store and download "This Naked Mind Companion App" and you can join the free alcohol experiment class whenever is a good time for you. https://apps.apple.com/gb/app/this-naked-mind-companion-app/id1616933854".[47] It really could be life changing! As you move forward into a more positive place in which excitement, elation and freedom begins to pervade your life *without* alcohol, suddenly you can enjoy life's rich experiences once again for what they are. Rich experiences…

"Naked," as Annie calls it.

With my soul searching now complete concerning the hugely significant alcohol component of *My Perfect Storm* (see chapter 5), I was now ready to begin a quest of searching and resolving some of the other aspects that had adversely impacted my health; namely my eating habits, workaholism, my inability to say "no", over-exercising and poor sleep.

It was time to join the dots.

10

Joining the Dots

After what felt like an incredibly turbulent six weeks when it came to securing any help from medical practitioners, on the other side of the coin I had my sessions with Henrietta (that were incredibly beneficial), my ever improving-sleep quality, exercise, fresh air, good nutrition and a slower pace of life – all of which were helping to re-balance and bring replenishment to my nervous system. I started to enjoy my own company, something which previously would not have been a preference for me as an extrovert, but definitely was what I needed for my reboot. It was remarkable how quickly my Garmin watch recorded a drop in stress levels; however, the correlating change in how I felt mentally and emotionally was not forthcoming until sometime later. 'Fragile', 'vulnerable' and 'lacking confidence', were watchwords for many more weeks and months to come. The process was going to take a further twelve months, with small steps and daily prioritising regarding key areas of self-care.

Despite being on the up, the deeper "why?" questions continued to unsettle me… I began to explore avenues by way of conventional medicine, but additionally, through periphery routes of DNA science and functional medicine. My aim was to unpick, understand and ultimately prevent a repeat of this episode in my life. After all, prevention was surely better than cure?

It is in this chapter that I wish to describe my voyage of 'joining-the-dots'; where I discover the root causes that led to my declining physical and mental health in October 2020. Some of what I share may resonate with you. I examine genetic, biological and physiological setbacks that impinged on my health, as well as the power of 'choice' to form deep rooted patterns of thoughts, beliefs, behaviours and motivations. Let me first, however, outline how the presenting symptoms were addressed by the conventional medics – specifically the repeated blood clot, SVT and acute perimenopausal stress.

My partnership with mainstream medicine

The vulnerability that I seemed to have towards blood clots was concerning. If I were to have an accident during one of my high-impact sports, for example cycling, skiing, or horse-riding, administering the blood thinning medication to my body could potentially lead to internal and external bleeding. The thought that this approach could end up being more life threatening concerned me, so I pursued a consultation with a haematologist. Multiple blood tests were taken to look at my propensity towards blood clots and although the results did not reveal a genetic predisposition, neither did they give me the green light to proceed without some type of anti-coagulant.[48] All the tests simply indicated, was that I was 'borderline' in terms of requiring long-term blood thinning medication and (in the haematologist's opinion) a low dose of Apixaban would suffice.

From a cardiology perspective, with my private 'outpatient' allowance exhausted for 2020, I couldn't make a private appointment with a cardiologist until early 2021. The Covid backlog in the NHS (National Health Service), indicated I would not be seen for several months… All I knew at this point, was that my heart was showing a very irregular ECG pattern and further intervention was likely to be required.

Following an initial consultation with the consultant cardiologist, I was booked in to undergo three to four weeks continuous ECG monitoring for February 2021. This involved continuously wearing a device with three electrodes on sticky patches, to record my heart rhythm. I also underwent an echocardiogram to scan my heart. Meanwhile, the cardiologist accessed the report that had been formulated from my forty-eight-hour ECG test, in September of 2020…

I vividly recall the day I went to receive my results, at my review consultation in March. The specialist came out into the waiting area and called my name. "Miss Fox?" he enquired, scanning the room. He couldn't seem to place me, so I left my seat and approached him.

"You have lost considerable weight, Miss Fox –" he said in a questioning tone. "How much have you lost?" I described that overall, I had lost 13 kg, but that since I had seen him in January, it had been 5 kg.

He was amazed and said, "That explains some of the changes I see between the two ECG read-outs…

"The one in October indicates acute SVT and the one now indicates a very negligible issue that does not require treatment. Your change in lifestyle, nutrition and the elimination of alcohol from your system, has completely reversed your SVT."

I was well-chuffed! The specialist went on to re-enforce that it was wise to continue with my alcohol-free choice for overall heart health and function and discharged me back to my GP with a clean bill of health. At this point, I was starting to draw significant conclusions regarding my recovery:

- Following my *Lumen* nutrition plans was working.
- 'Hacking my metabolism' was working.
- Having the right balance of exercise was important.
- Significant fat loss was extremely beneficial.
- Eliminating alcohol was crucial.
- Maintaining good sleep was essential.
- If the above were in order, then lower stress levels were inevitable.

I plant a 'high-five' to the 'conventional' medical team for their knowledge and their efficient technology, partnering with me to confirm that I was on the right tracks in my journey to healing and recovery.

I had successfully achieved the directive: To reverse a developing heart irregularity. I was beginning to feel such an incredible sense of relief! Whilst I still needed to remain on a low dose of apixaban, my heart was fine, and I was beginning to feel the benefits of HRT for perimenopausal stress. Perhaps there was light beginning to appear at the end of this tunnel?

My partnership with non-conventional healthcare

Circle by DNAfit[49]

In December 2020, I got onboard "Circle" – a product by award-winning health and wellness company *DNAfit*, which facilitates personal DNA testing to provide an overall personal report on your DNA, using the latest in scientific innovation. It takes DNA testing into a very detailed space, in terms of evaluating genetic predisposition, uniquely offering tests sent directly from the lab to the comfort of your home.

When I received my tests back, it provided results regarding the following:

- My diet and lifestyle with regards to nutrition, well-being, stress, sleep, the effect of pollution and my skin.
- My talent and sports performance – including sports I participate in, fitness, success traits, music, and dance.
- My ancestry composition.
- My genetic blueprint – including personality traits, behavioural traits, physical traits and gender traits.

It also provided a detailed analysis on the following, although not all were applicable:

- "Protect your Family" – including family planning.
- "Early Detection" – including reports on cancer risk, dementia and brain health.
- "Health and Disease" – including common health risks as well as chronic disease risk.
- "Precision medicine" (or 'personalised medicine'): A tailored medicinal response that goes beyond the *one-size-fits-all* prevalent with most medical treatments.

The results were interesting on a number of levels, not least because they were incredibly accurate (regarding some of the physical traits determined by genetics). Some I found amusing! They were the results that came back reading,

- "Persistent Thinness - *less likely thin*"
- "Waist Circumference - *likely larger*"

I laugh out loud every time! By reading my DNA, *Circle* were able to tell me my eye and hair colour, my pain sensitivity threshold, even my body odour (yuk)! All were uncannily accurate (and needless to say, I smell like roses)!

The engaging information that accompanied the data underpinning the "Persistent Thinness" gene in my *personal DNA report*, is as follows:

> *"There is a reason why slim parents have slim children and the same with overweight parents [although not always]. Persistent thinness [defined as individuals who have a BMI < 18.5 kg/m2 consistently] has been found to be a heritable trait, just like severe obesity. In fact, around 40-70% of our weight is determined by our genetics."*

It further explains, how those with the genetic predisposition towards either end of the scale, may either struggle to lose or gain weight, depending on which way they lean. However, it also highlights that importantly, *lifestyle and environment* have a big impact on an individual being thin (specifically). In other words, a person may have a specific predisposition, but this does not have to determine their 'genetic expression'.[50]

I do not have the scope to discuss "genetic disposition" and "genetic expression" in detail here; suffice to say that your lifestyle choices can enable you to express your DNA differently. As someone with two genes that predispose me to being a lot larger than I am, although I once fit my genetic predisposition 'bill', my life now is a testimony to the truth of transformative lifestyle choices.

Through my DNA test, the answers I was searching for were coming in thick and fast. As I understood my biological and physiological makeup and their predisposition to stress etc, the results also highlighted the reaction of my emotional and mental states. They really do go hand-in-hand. It would be possible for me to write a paper on the entirety of my DNA results, but they are of little relevance to you as the reader. As it did with me, knowing your unique genetics may both signpost you to understand why your propensity leans towards certain responses, and additionally, enable you to make informed lifestyle choices that better support your overall well-being. If you're curious about what your own test results might yield, then follow this link which is also available on my website in the Resources section:

https://dnafit.com/cart/DNAFIT-X-PRO-FIT-DIRECT/1/gbp/MariaFoxAffiliate

Thankfully, whilst I am now incredibly metabolically flexible, I am looking towards a five-year goal of sustained weight loss, as that will truly be indicative of having re-wired my metabolism, (therefore my lifestyle), to support my physical health for the long-term.

Gut Microbiome[51] and Adrenal Gland Function[52]

In early February 2021, a good friend of mine called Sara (whom I have known since 1997 and features in the endorsement section) found out through a mutual friend that I was unwell. She was less than impressed that I had not been in touch, my only real excuse being that she was a busy Deputy Chief Constable in Hampshire Constabulary, and I was playing the introvert for a change!

After a preliminary catch-up through the wonders of a video facetime call, we met at a service station on the UK's M1. I brought her up-to-date with where I was at in life and with her well-being expertise, she recommended that I explore my gut microbiome health, together with an Adrenal Glands test, suggesting a provider called *Healthpath.*[53] As a company who specialise in functional medicine, Sara expressed that this platform might also provide insights into how badly I may have damaged myself, how well I was recovering, and give me valuable information about securing the right type of supplement protocol to help me to optimise my recovery. She was impressed with the progress I had made to date and all the things I was embracing from a nutrition, exercise, sleep and stress management perspective. However, this next level of exploration (namely gut microbiome and Adrenal Glands testing) were two aspects I would not have come across, had it not been for Sara.

So... Why gut microbiome and Adrenal Gland function? Firstly, gut microbiome is so important because research suggests it supports the following five body functions:

1. Immune function
2. Heart health and cholesterol regulation
3. Brain health
4. The control of blood sugar and lowering the risk of Diabetes
5. Regulation of weight. (Preventing weight gain, which can happen through gut dysbiosis.[54])

If you would like to learn more, I recommend reading a short article by healthline, which you can find in the endnotes.[55] Additionally, Dr Gerard Mullins' book, *The Gut Balance Revolution*, is another good read, offering you an approach on 'resetting your gut' over a three-month period, without undertaking any tests. However, if you like the idea of testing, you can use a provider like *Healthpath or Zoe Health*, which will help you to address your specifics. I have read many articles that indicate good gut health as one of the more significant factors, when it comes to weight loss. We can have good nutrition, good sleep, healthy stress levels and a good degree of activity, but if you are suffering from 'gut dysbiosis', you simply will not shed fat.

By the time I underwent my gut microbiome test, I had lost a significant amount of fat. However, I wanted to ensure that my gut had the right levels of good bacteria to promote a 'healthy gut microbiome'. (You may need to look up some of these words, or alternatively visit Healthpath.com.)

As was suspected, I had work to do…

Turning attention to the Adrenal Gland function, above what my gut microbiome health may have been, Sara's bigger concern was the prospect of 'adrenal fatigue'; that I may have damaged my adrenal function indefinitely. I trusted what Sara had to say, because as a soon to be functional medicine practitioner, she knew her stuff. I wanted to make sure I had all bases covered in order to recover well and be strong again. So, I decided to also have an assessment of my Adrenal Glands.

This test examines cortisol and DHEA[56] levels. Cortisol levels naturally fluctuate throughout the day, and I was required to provide five samples to show my body's cortisol rhythm. By measuring levels of cortisol and DHEA, it is possible to assess how a person's body responds to stress. The results provided both a morning and evening DHEA analysis and then an expertly designed adrenal health diet and lifestyle plan.

My test result levels indicated someone either about to enter a place of chronic fatigue and burnout, or someone who was in the process of recovering. (In other words, the levels would be akin to either pre, or post-burnout.) From my symptom questionnaire and history, it was clear that I was on the road to recovery. I was given a bespoke supplement protocol (just as Sara had said) and lifestyle recommendations, as I continued to work towards my goal. Although at this stage, it was still hard to assess whether I would make a full recovery in terms of my ability to manage high levels of stress again. It would indeed be many months later that I would witness my mental and emotional resilience notably returning.

Mindset resources to support my recovery

My trip to the Police treatment centre at Harrogate as a participant on their Psychological Well-being programme, was key at this point of my journey, as were two books I listened to, which were really helpful. The first was *Switch on Your Brain*, by Christian neuroscientist Dr Caroline Leaf.[57] It was encouraging to listen to a 'self-help' book by an author and scientist who held the same faith beliefs as me. From my perspective it was a more complex read, but absolutely brilliant.

Leaf navigates the reader into understanding how our choices change our brain's neurological pathways. She explains how the mind controls matter, describing also how we can 'detox our brains' in order to be fully switched on every day and re-invigorated, to support a healthy lifestyle. My main take-away from this book was to consider my thought-life and how my choice of meditations could impact my well-being for the better (or for the worse). The "21 Day Brain Detox Plan" contained within this book is also a great approach to deconflict and reset your computer's main- frame.

The second book was Dr Libby Weaver's book, *Rushing Woman Syndrome*, which I've mentioned in a previous chapter. She writes with incredible insight about the impact 'rushing' has on our mental and emotional well-being. As I listened, it felt like she had written the book just for me… It was crucial timing as I considered the next phase of my journey, which was to return to work.

Libby made all the complex scientific and interconnected processes very simple to understand, encouraging me, like *Lumen* and *Healthpath*, to dig deep, evaluate my behaviours and beliefs and what was at the root of all the 'rushing' in the first place. *What* exactly had I been trying to prove? *Who* was I trying to prove *what* to? Why was I a "people-pleaser"? What impact was people-pleasing having on my health? And how was I going to learn to use the 'two-letter-word' more frequently – firstly to take care of myself, and secondly, (yet not subordinately), to walk in truth? How was I going to learn to use the word "No"?

I knew I had to take on the challenge. With the word "no" tucked into my belt and ensuring I didn't over-reach myself in the days and weeks to come, I started to believe I could get there.

I felt ready.

It was time to re-engage with people and navigate my return to work.

11

Get Back on That Horse!

A Return-to-Work Transition

Psychologically, the prospect of returning to work was quite a daunting one, for numerous reasons. Lack of confidence and insecurity… What did people think and what would they be saying? What was the narrative being advocated? Notwithstanding these thoughts, the overriding and deepest fear I carried was returning to the place where mentally, emotionally and physically I would decline again – if not immediately, then over time. It was inconceivable that I could *ever* go through anything like this again, especially now I was so far along the road to recovery. This meant that the process and transition to rehabilitation was crucial; and whilst I had certainly gone above and beyond on a personal level to make right my health, including investing a great deal of personal finance into private health acquisition, menopause specialists, functional medicine approaches, and DNA testing, I simply could not allow myself to be in a position where history might repeat itself.

I give mention from the outset that my employer, West Midlands Police (WMP), were exceptional in this regard. With the support of Occupational Health specialists (notably Henrietta) and the Force Medical Examiner, alongside the Head of People, Nicola Price, I was managed back into the workplace (and duly back into my Senior leadership role), in the best possible way. If my voyage could be captured as a case study for other organisations to gain from, I would recommend learning from WMP, whom I give a five-star rating to. If there was to be a paper titled *'How to Effectively Manage an Employee Back into Full and Productive Delivery: Ensuring a successful transition back into the workplace, to benefit both employee and employer'*, WMP would be exemplary. It is true that every thriving workplace starts from the attitude of those at the helm, placing the emphasis rather than on an organisation per se, to people instead: Key individuals and relationships, (so make sure you've got good ones in yours). WMP created the right process, because it was implemented by the right people – and they took incredible care of me.

There were, what I will describe as, several 'phases' for my transition back to work, until I reached the point where I was able to say I was 100% fully fit and well again. The remainder of this chapter outlines this return-to-work transition.

Phase 1 – Contemplating a return to work

In early 2021, the suggestion of getting "back on that horse" – even the thought – really scared me and made me incredibly anxious. I shrank back into a place of overwhelm very quickly, which was indicative to me that my mental and emotional capacity was at a low ebb. The event that triggered this episode was when my line manager contacted me. I had somehow given him the impression that I was going to return to work in the New Year, over some dialogue we had exchanged prior to Christmas. I cannot remember what I said to give him this impression, but I must have verbalised *something* to cause him to believe my return was imminent.

On New Year's Eve, he sent me a text message asking if I was available to speak. I began to break out in a sweat! How should I reply? I wasn't contemplating the notion at all! Aside from my panic, I realised he genuinely thought I was returning and was just simply trying to be organised. That said, I still needed to communicate to him that I was not feeling anywhere near ready to return to work. I was still feeling extremely fragile, not knowing if I'd be capable of ever returning to the role I had been in prior to all of this…after all, it had only been just over two months since everything had caved in around me. So, I declined the request to speak and asked if he would contact me come the New Year.

Unsurprisingly, with the statement "in the New Year" being interpreted by the general population as January 1st onwards, my line manager keenly contacted me. Before the first week was out, he had messaged a few times asking to discuss the aforementioned subject. I reluctantly agreed to have a conversation, albeit betwixt progressing a private cardiologist appointment and resolving an acute dental issue (timing)! He wanted to ask my views on changing the structure and composition of portfolios on the senior leadership team, by proposing he divide my portfolio. Whilst hearing the words "dividing my portfolio" was along the right track, the reality for me at this stage was that I couldn't foresee whether I would be well enough to ever work in policing again, let alone return to the context that had been conducive to my decline in the first place.

At this juncture, I was still trying to navigate a haematologist, cardiologist and gynaecologist to address the physical challenges my body was experiencing. The HR business manager had agreed to be my welfare officer and as such, I explained that I did not feel ready, nor able to consider returning to my post. What I needed, was to give myself permission to recover in the way my body, soul and spirit were crying out for. And so, I asked my welfare officer if she would ensure that for the time-being, there would be no further contact regarding the terms by which I would be returning to work.

Henceforth, I explored the turmoil I was feeling concerning my return to work with my counsellor. As a result of our session, I concluded it was simply not a safe context to host an effective recovery, due to the intensity of the physical and mental trauma associated with it.

This was a turning point for me. I share about it, because it applies to so much in life; with how we navigate change and from our innate instinct to self-preserve. As such, I'd like to expand on this topic slightly. The "primitive" brain does four things to protect us. It

1. conserves energy;
2. avoids pain, discomfort and anything that doesn't feel good;
3. pursues gratification, i.e., the things that keep us alive, (e.g., food, relationships, reproduction);
4. proves itself right, meaning that it seeks to make predictions on what's happened, based on experience. (It prefers to predetermine, rather than step into the unknown.)

It is typically why humans say, "Well, we've always done it this way," or "We used to do…" (this or that). We are creatures of habit and whilst this is good for establishing healthy routines in our life, it is also a reason why people can be resistant to change. The pain of staying the same, must be more acute than the challenge of change; likewise, the *benefits* of change need to outweigh the pros of staying the same, if we are to embrace change. Putting this into context, my brain was both trying to protect me from re-entering an environment where previously I had experienced harm, whilst at the same time, weighing up the pros and cons of change. The issue was that I feared I would simply revert back into old habits, leading to another downward spiral.

I resolved, after much deliberation, that in order to return to the working environment, I needed a different role – a fresh start, in order that I could begin rebuilding my confidence and re-establishing myself.

I was unsure how exactly to navigate this via Occupational Health, but I started off by doing what I perceived to be the decent thing, which was to let my line manager know my intentions. Whilst he accepted all of what I had to say and in an understanding manner, it backfired a little when he relayed this to his superiors! I found myself on the receiving end of a request to detail my full rationale for not wanting to return to my former role and to provide feedback on the department and issues therein! Logical for long-term learning, but positively unhelpful to someone with presently limited emotional and mental resilience! I chose not to respond and simply outlined my position formally in writing, via my welfare officer. It was an uncomfortable couple of weeks – a blip in my otherwise steady progress, but also necessary so that in due course, the right plans could be put in place and supported by Occupational Health.

Phase 2 – The preparation phase

In the last chapter *Joining the Dots, a*ll that took place during that time is what this phase encompassed. To add to it, I asked Vanessa during one of our weekly calls whether she thought it would be appropriate for me to approach Nicola Price, (Head of People and Organisational Development), for a conversation regarding my return to work and to discuss my role and transition. (This was some time on following the 'blip' in Phase 1.) Vanessa line managed Nicola and suggested that I email her.

It was early Spring, 2021, when I fixed a meeting with Nicola at WMP Headquarters. By the time of our meeting, I had been reviewed by the Force Medical Examiner (Force M.E.), who clarified his role [on my return] as the 'recommendation officer' with regards to my environment and working hours, supplementing this with a list of all the things that were very important, relating to sustaining my health improvements. Whilst this was reassuring, I was nervous about seeing Nicola... So, I prepared a full written report of my journey to clearly explain the context, along with all of the various challenges that I felt I was facing presently.

I arrived at Lloyd house. Nicola was quite taken aback at the weight I had lost since she had last seen me, commenting on how much better I was looking. We bought a coffee and sat down to chat... She was warm, receptive and made me feel comfortable, enabling me to be very open and honest about my health, my ongoing recovery, and my overall policing experience. She clearly understood the complex mix of factors that had contributed to my ill-health. She listened, suggesting that I go away and describe back to her what would be my ideal short-term and longer-term posting to facilitate my transition.

I consulted on this with both Sam and Vanessa, who both knew me well and who were able to provide some helpful perspectives on both a realistic and a step-by-step approach. I submitted my 'ideals' to Nicola, which she accepted. I went ahead and had a "fit-to-return" letter signed by my GP and the Force M.E., who recommended a 'managed'[58] return protocol. Meanwhile, I took all of my outstanding annual leave from the 2020/21 year and returned officially to the workplace on Tuesday 5th May, 2021 – just shy of six months out of the workplace. Nicola had put in place a short-term plan for me to work in People and Organisational

Development[59] supporting the Recruitment Uplift Programme,[60] with responsibility for developing and implementing two specific initiatives: Recruitment Ambassadors[61] and a Summer Academy[62] for young people.

It was official. I was now returning to work,

Phase 3 – Force M.E. phased transition

The Force M.E. agreed a phased transition from May 5th into late August 2021. It was a slow, but wise and incremental build-up starting with four hours a day, every other day. This then built up to six hours, then again gradually until a full eight hours were reached. With Wednesdays off routinely every week to serve as a buffer, it was a programme that worked extremely well. There were, however, days when I wondered if I would ever regain my previous levels of mental and emotional resilience, for even just one meeting would leave me feeling exhausted. But I took hold of hope… that as my physical health had taken incredible shape over a period of just seven months, so I would see my soul healing and resilience begin to return.

The Psychological Well-being course was fast approaching and proved to be a brilliant recommendation for this phase of my transition. Taking place at the Police Treatment Centre in Harrogate, it was like an oasis in a desert! With excellent accommodation and amazing facilities typical of a spa, we were offered complimentary therapy treatments, physiotherapy, relaxation lounges, gym classes, good food, and so much more. During this time-out, I gained a deeper perspective and clarity regarding many things, including how, as Sam progressed through the Chief Superintendent selection process in WMP, there was no way *in a million years* I could ever put myself in that kind of context again! I was, of course, overjoyed for Sam when she received the news that she had been successful! As for me, I was just simply relieved that I was starting to improve…that it was looking increasingly optimistic my being on target to finish my policing service successfully and with some pride.

The well-being programme itself offered multiple workshops, including how to deal with trauma and stress, developing awareness, understanding nutrition, tips for relaxation, the healing aroma of essential oils and more, as well as counselling sessions if desired. The focus was to support attendees in both their short and long-term 'well-being journeys', providing tools and strategies so that once back in the workplace, one was better equipped to manage.

✣ ✣ ✣

Back to work, I was feeling more positive and very fortunate to be working with Nicola and Lucia Leon, leader of the programme I was assigned to. Lucia was incredibly supportive, competent and organised. Her enthusiasm and commitment, together with retaining emotional awareness, made Lucia fantastic to work with. She was the perfect project manager for someone like me; someone who needed to feel safe and confident at stepping back into my extrovert personality. Like a flower, Lucia helped me to open up so that once more, I could begin to blossom in my people skills. I returned swiftly into establishing rapports, engaging with and motivating others, all of which was hugely important in my new role.

Although I felt very out of my comfort zone at times, she gave me all the tools I required to shape the delivery of the Recruitment Ambassadors initiative and the Summer Academy for that year. Lucia, myself and Inspector Wes Smith, worked together to develop the programme, going on to deliver what was an incredibly successful three-day event for a group of nine Year 11's from a local Duddeston school. I felt like I was beginning to find myself in the workplace again...

As a result of the Summer Academy's success, I wrote a blog for our internal news thread (*Humans of WMP*[63]). Whilst not quite ready to be loud and proud, I was beginning to see how my journey and all that I had learned through it might help individuals finding themselves either heading towards, or in, a similar place.

So, I was now coming to the end of my four-month transition. All the way through I had been supported by regular catchups with Nicola, which proved to be a vital component in the transition process. As August was drawing to a close and we looked forward to where I would be for September and beyond, I was asked to preference a formal posting. I provided several options including Local Policing, Operations and Professional Standards and shortly afterwards was posted to Local Policing at Sandwell NPU,[64] as the Local Policing Superintendent.

The next phase of my journey was about to begin…

✣ ✣ ✣

Albeit sensing in my 'Noah' that I was not back to what I knew was my best or strongest self, I felt ready to take this next step. I was making good progress and knew that if I was disciplined in sustaining my health improvements, (i.e., the Four Pillars[65]), anything was possible. The extraordinary physical health transformation I experienced was such a powerful indicator of what was possible and, knowing that my new line manager, Ian Green, was a man who took care of his people, I was confident that I would be positioned in the best possible environment in which to flourish.

To "flourish" in my book, meant being confident as a senior leader and able to create an environment in which all team members could be their best in serving local communities. What I didn't anticipate, was the magnitude at which I went from strength to strength – so much so, that in March of 2022, I would be knocking on the door of a promotion opportunity.

12

Carpe Diem - Seize the Day

Twenty-twenty-two was my year of *Carpe diem*[66] – of making the most of every opportunity, as my mental and emotional resilience took flight and started to soar. It was a truly incredible journey; many important treasures were discovered and picked up along the way.

As I sail now across a new ocean, I stand at the side of my ship throwing gifts to you; gifts that offer knowledge; gifts that have transformed my life.

The gift of creating new muscle memory, to help sustain health and well-being

The first gift I wish to offer, especially if you are someone undergoing a transition in your life, is to make sure you look after yourself well. The "Four Pillars" I named in the *Introduction* as 'Nutrition', 'Movement', 'Sleep' and 'Stress Management', are the key components to assess where any bad habits are in situ and the places to begin considering where new habits need to be formed. As I consider my own journey in the act of demolishing old muscle memories and creating new ones, it really takes discipline and determination. I felt it several times upon entering back into my busy police Superintendent role. To learn to adjust back into a work setting, whilst still managing to embrace and prioritise the Four Pillars, was the task.

I am sure you understand the terminology 'muscle memory', however, please let me indulge by giving an analogy I rather like and that helped me a lot as a concept and visual aid when it came to changing bad habits. I like to use the analogy of a game of tennis, because it requires great agility and flexibility. Let me explain. For those of you who know the sport, you'll agree that it's easy to play forehand when the ball lands repeatedly in front of you. Not a great deal of movement is required, and one barely works up a sweat. What makes it more difficult, is when the ball is played out wide, or played high. In this scenario, you need to be constantly manoeuvring your position in order to make the best strike. Similarly, in terms of learning and the brain, the way the muscle memory improves for any of us, in any given area, is challenging the established muscle memory with different contexts. Specifically, in order to change and improve, you need to challenge yourself with something slightly different each time (thus 'position' yourself differently). Akin to weightlifting, if you pick up the same weights in the same body position each time, whilst you'll develop the targeted area, you won't experience much muscle development beyond that.

With the gift of muscle memory shared, I would like to describe how it impacted the Four Pillars. I refer to each pillar as a 'treasure' that I discovered along the course of my journey.

† *Treasure nutrition* †

When I consider what my eating habits were like, my entire police service characteristically stated, 'poor nutrition'. The only time when there had been any type of consistency was in the very early days, when we had police canteens, and even though we might often get turned out on a job,[67] at least we had a place where we could buy healthy (or unhealthy) food and sit together to eat.

As my time and role in the service became more demanding, so I began eating more and more in front of a computer to get jobs done, or on the run from one place to another. As I contemplated this lifestyle, I knew it was going to take a renewing of my mind and intentional physical changes to create new muscle memory. I knew (as with every bad habit I needed to break), I would have to be alert so as not to fall back into old ways. Until my new eating habits were ingrained and second nature, I therefore decided to schedule a daily plan in my electronic diary.

Having a diary really helped me keep a check on myself, making sure I was incorporating proper break times and good nutritious meals during my time at work. My diet would be along the lines of eggs, spinach and avocado for breakfast, which would really set me up for the day. Other food was relatively quick to get together – usually chicken or king prawns with spinach in a wholemeal pitta bread at lunchtime and a protein bar for mid-morning or afternoon snack.

Thankfully, I adjusted to my new routine quickly and it soon became a natural rhythm in my daily life. Once I reached 2022, I felt the diary slots were no longer needed and I was confident that the new routines were now well-established. My new muscle memory with regards to nutrition, had been created.

† *Treasure movement* †

It is incredibly important to keep moving; to have some form of exercise and movement each day. For myself as a sports junkie, I thought this might be a more challenging habit to break than my diet, because I could so easily get lost in the moment and push myself too far. This is where the vital pillar of sleep and a properly thought-out routine comes in.

I always liked to do exercise first thing in the morning, so as soon as I got my sleeping to a place where it was quality, it was as simple as planning my day to make sure I could get my morning dose. I concluded that I needed to be in bed very early, (by 9 pm), in order to be up for 5 am (or thereabouts).

With my sleep established, I had a few options when it came to incorporating my morning drill. I made the plan to exercise on my *Stages* indoor bicycle at least two mornings a week, before heading to work. The other days, I could either get up early and do an outdoor ride, or cycle to work. (Even cycle in extra early, if I wanted to fit in weight training when I got back home.) As I experimented, I found the best rhythm that worked for me was to be flexible, as per my work requirements.

Over the initial twelve months, I found the best options and variations to work consistently around each other. New muscle memory with regards to exercise, had also now been created.

† *Treasure sleep* †

I have already mentioned the significance of developing a healthy and proper sleep routine. Sleeping between the recommended hours, as determined by experts, is essential, regardless of whether you are in work or not. Scientists have found that between the hours of 10 pm and 2 am, your 'central computer' concentrates on restoring your physical condition, while the subsequent four hours thereafter focuses on unravelling and restoring your emotional side.

Once you have a correct sleep pattern and rest rhythm established, it will not be long until your body-clock adjusts and you'll probably not even need an alarm to get up in the mornings. This is an excellent routine to establish, because it supports the body and metabolism to function optimally into a natural circadian rhythm.[68] I have noticed how much my sleep quality consistently scores mid to high eighties (out of one hundred) on my Garmin connect data. When it slips, I take measures to address; however, by-and-large the muscle memory regarding my new sleep routine, is fully established.

Food wise, it is recommended not to eat close to bedtime and to minimise carbohydrates in the evening, as both can elevate cortisol levels, (which also impacts sleep quality as we learned in chapter 2).

† Treasure less-stress †

Gaining an understanding of what impacts stress levels, is crucial. For myself, prayer and reflection played a huge part in helping me keep stress levels to a minimum, along with prioritising quality sleep, amending my hectic exercise regimes, and addressing my diet. This is where I have found my Garmin watch to be incredibly useful. I used my G-Fenix 7S to track my responses to multiple stimuli and it's helped me no end with making the best decisions, with regards to health and well-being. I am sure some folk will think that my constant data tracking is a little obsessive! However, the *Lumen* and Garmin gadgets have proven themselves to be fantastic health and wellness partners.

With these four *treasures* taken hold of and nurtured, I can confidently say that over twelve months later (and still more), I have not only been able to integrate a healthy lifestyle into my working life, but sustain it.

The gift of a good line manager

After all I had been through, I have learned how important it is to have a supportive line manager. Ian Green was (and still is) a very straightforward and uncomplicated leader. He is definitely a ‹what you see is what you get' kind-a guy. He is open, transparent, thoughtful and direct, but very caring along with it. He understands people and policing; that a healthy workforce, means a high performing workforce. Ian's ethos, much like my own, is that if you look after people the right way, then they are going to deliver the best results and serve to the best of their ability. In my years of experience as a senior leader, people who are healthy and know that you care, deliver well and will go the extra mile. *People don't care how much you know, until they know how much you care.* A good line manager truly is a gift. If *you* are a line manager, be the gift of a good one.

Well, August and September passed, and October 2021 arrived. The twelve-month 'anniversary' for *That Sunday Afternoon* was steadily approaching. As the 25th arrived, suddenly the download of memory recall cascaded, opening a torrent of emotions that didn't pass as the day ended. The 26th came and went…the 27th and so on.

We headed into November, and I was still struggling to shake it off, with dreams tormenting me at night. I alerted Ian and reached out to Henrietta, asking if this was a normal part of the process. Seeing as I had never experienced anything like this before, I thought it was wise to be open about what was going on and how I was feeling. She explained that it was fairly normal, especially in the early 'anniversaries' of traumatic events, being akin to experiencing a bereavement or a tragedy and encouraged me to reach out if it continued to repeat itself.

You know, sometimes, it's just the simple act of understanding what is going on that can help us take huge steps forward. *Scientia potentia est*[69] – with knowledge comes power (and with power, great responsibility).[70]

With knowledge, can also come peace; once I *knew* that this was a normal process, I was able to come to terms with it. With this understanding, I would be able to prepare myself for [what could be] the annual event.

By the time Christmas had arrived, I was beginning to feel more like myself again. With gratitude, I got through my first major emotional blip. It had the potential to derail my progress but with the ability to be open with Ian and Henrietta I was soon back on track.

The gift of a new start

When you nurture the gifts and receive the treasure, another is given to you: the gift of a new start. This gift needs to be carefully guarded, so not to be stolen…

I was easing back into the groove of local policing and my responsibilities as a uniform Superintendent. Keen to get back onto the Tactical Firearms Commander[71] rota (TFC), I looked to secure my position on a training course. It was an area where I had sought re-accreditation as it was a previous responsibility that I had enjoyed. I could feel myself getting stronger, both mentally and physically, so felt I was up for the task.

As 2022 commenced, I was also finding myself motivated concerning my career beyond policing. Scott Pinyard had reached out to me from *This Naked Mind Institute* (TNMI) and asked if I had considered their coaching course, which I replied to with a resounding "Yes!" I had been mentoring in the monthly *Live Alcohol Experiment* for the past twelve months and enjoying living effortlessly free of the substance. It felt like the next stage for me.

The content of the course looked amazing, and I decided it was too great an opportunity to miss. The introductory immersion event did not disappoint either! Although it was facilitated online via the videotelephony application *Zoom* (*Zoom Video Communications Inc.*), which can make things incredibly impersonal, the way in which Annie Grace and Scott facilitated, enabled me to feel as though I was actually there. It was an amazing forty-eight hours (with breaks in-between!) and I had a feeling the next six months was going to be an amazing journey of personal growth.

In my book, the timing was perfect.

All was well. I had time and space to focus on personal development at work with my initial TFC course about to commence and my weekly coaching material to work through. I was amazed at my continually increasing resilience. Enter stage right…. The opportunity to apply for a temporary Chief Superintendent selection process.

Uh-oh…

Was I about to slip back into old ways of starting to spin too many plates again? I pondered for a while and made the decision that I was *not* about to jeopardise my health, even though I sensed the time was right for me to push the promotion door. How was I going to negotiate this without compromising my well-being?

As I reflected that my previous approach would have sought to manage all aspects simultaneously, (i.e., spin all those plates at the same time), my thoughts turned to whether I could focus on each one *in turn*, rather than needing to withdraw from any one of them completely. I took the opportunity during my coaching call with Scott to explore the option of pausing full participation in the weekly content for TNMI until the other priorities had been finalised. Hurrah! There was no pressing deadline, so I was free to catch up anything I missed at a later stage. One plate put down… With this on hold, I felt able to run with the TFC course and prepare myself for the Temporary Chief Superintendent interview at WMP.

Thankfully, it was a favourable strategy; my well-being had not been compromised. The interview came and went. It wasn't the first time I had undertaken a selection process for chief superintendent, but this time had reflected afterwards that I had played my 'best set', acquitting myself well. I had long recognised that perimenopausal short-term memory losses might undermine any interview performance, but for me this was by far my best shot to date. Although the vacancies were not fully determined at this stage, I received feedback to say, "I had done myself proud" and that was enough for me. Whether I was appointed to a temporary Chief Superintendent role or otherwise, I felt a sense of satisfaction and optimism that I might be afforded an opportunity at the next substantive selection process.

I progressed in April and May to undertake and pass both Initial and Cadre TFC courses whilst resuming full participation on the TNMI coaching course. By early July, I had completed the programme, submitted multiple written and practical assignments for assessment and successfully secured my TNMI coaching accreditation. In the very same week, I also received the news that I was now being promoted to Temporary Chief Superintendent at Sandwell, in Ian's stead! That day got marked down as a poignant moment in my life, which I will never forget. This incredible journey of both health transformation, personal rediscovery and growth, had led me to this; to a place of being successful in a way that I could not have anticipated. I thanked Ian and wished him all the best as he prepared to move on to his new role.

✣ ✣ ✣

The academic year of 21/22 had seen me bounce back to full health, as well as enjoy the satisfaction of several achievements I would not have imagined possible the previous year. I was feeling buoyed, motivated and inspired in all areas of my life.

In closing this sub-section, I would like to say this: *Guard your new life.* Don't allow it to be stolen from you. *Share your scars but not your wounds.*[72] Keep those good people around you, whom you can turn to when the negative sneaks up behind and tries to jump on you or push you through a back door. Stay open and accountable. Gain knowledge, to unlock the power to overcome and be empowered to mentally prepare.

The gift of imparting to others

Something I love to do is pass on to other people things I have learned. I love to see individuals being empowered and to be part of that process is a privilege. Life throws us curveballs at times…but every single one of them presents an opportunity for us to learn, grow from, and help others who may be going through a similar situation. I hope you have found these 'gifts' to be wisdom and knowledge that you can embrace because *life* is a gift and should indeed be treasured.

As I stood at the gateway of 2023 with the completed manuscript of this book in hand and ready for the editor to take onboard, there is no question that his rounds off what has been an incredible journey from *Crisis to Comeback.*

CARPE DIEM folks! Don't wait to make the changes that are in your power to make!

Conclusion

The next phase of my journey is yet to be written. Some will say, "Why did you not wait to write your book *post* your policing career? Why did you take on this project *now*? How on earth did you find the time?!"

I felt compelled to write whilst still a serving officer and, for leaders serving in policing, frontline police officers and staff as well as others outside of policing in high demand working contexts; individuals who may be heading for a burnout episode or trying to recover from one. If I had written this book as a retired senior police officer, I would have been distanced from both the season in my life that is the subject matter, as well as the context in which I experienced and learned so much.

It is a prose written with one eye on the past and one on the future: remembering the pain and discomfort that pressed me into exponential personal growth, which is important never to forget, and also looking to what my life beyond policing might look like. When this time comes, I might be primarily stationed as a health and well-being consultant, in a position from all I have learned and gained, to present credible coaching from a foundation of 'lived experience'.

With a desire to equip, prevent and rescue individuals from burnout, this book releases a message of hope, as well as providing practical options for self-care to those within policing, and also other high stress environments and roles. It is a 'roadmap' pointing the way to health and wellness, and a path leading to restoration in the event of the worst happening. Hearing of and seeing so many colleagues lose their battle for life and so young, as a result of chronic diseases such as cancer, sudden cardiac events, blood clots, pulmonary embolisms – even suddenly dying whilst in service – has also been another impetus for me writing this book. Whether we want to acknowledge it or not, research indicates that consistently high stress levels, 24/7 shifts and shift-working per se, alongside sleep deprivation, long working hours and regular alcohol consumption all serve to increase our risk of chronic ill health. And this is *before* considering the impact of that trauma, inherent in our working roles, has on our nervous system…

All of these things create a toxic cycle for cellular health and it is why we need to prioritise, what I have referred to throughout this book, as the Four Pillars: Nutrition, Movement (exercise), Sleep and Stress/mindset Management. Genetic predisposition is a prominent factor in perhaps as few as 5% of those who find themselves facing chronic disease, but for the remainder of us, research suggests that battling such diseases will be a result of the combination and cumulation of lifestyle choices and environment.

I hope, having shared my heart, my vulnerability, my weaknesses and my scars, alongside my determination and tenacity to make changes, that you will be inspired to take steps to prioritise your own health and well-being. Likewise, if you are a leader, to support your friends and family as well as your colleagues and those you have charge over.

Policing is a relentless role and I know that whilst many of us thrive in the career vocation we have chosen, and indeed have loved every minute, it is important to make sure we pay attention to self-care and reduce the pace of our lives for the sake of longevity. None of us are invincible and take it from me – it is better *not* to discover that the hard way!

If you have enjoyed this book, please drop me a line! You can follow me on Instagram @livewelland_free, or subscribe to my growing YouTube channel @MariaFoxWellness, where you will find some videos on various themes linked to well-being. For further resources on nutrition, exercise, sleep, stress management, alcohol-free living and menopause, I invite you to visit my website, where I plan to make some downloadable pdfs available in due course. You can find it at *www.livewellandfree.co.uk*

If you would like to delve deeper into your health, resilience, and energy, Infinite8wellbeing offers a bespoke service including personal testing, genetics, naturopathic nutrition plans and health coaching delivered by trained experts, leaders with "lived experience", who have thrived in high stress and trauma environments. Contact sara@infinite8wellbeing.com

Finally, if you would like to invite me to speak or present on any of the subjects covered in my journey, you can contact me via my well-being email: *info@livewellandfree.co.uk* . As for this present moment, I leave the stage by penning these words…

Watch out for – and look after – each other.

Epilogue

In February 2023, after submitting this manuscript for the edit and proof-read process, Maria applied for, and was successful in the Derbyshire Constabulary Chief Superintendent promotion selection process.

In April 2023, she was formally offered a substantive Chief Superintendent role with Derbyshire Constabulary.

Carpe Diem folks! Make the small changes that you can today, apply some diligence to navigate the new path and in due course you will reap the rewards of all that you sow.

APPENDIX 1

Myths about Fat Loss

Fat loss is based on multiple factors, not simply nutrition. These same factors affect what your metabolism (your 'engine') *chooses* to use for fuel. Here are just some of those factors to consider in the complex process:

- greater output of energy usage compared to consumption
- healthy functioning mitochondria so that nutrition is converted to energy
- healthy gut microbiome
- good hormone balance / function
- normal cortisol levels [consistently elevated levels will prevent fat loss]
- normal insulin levels [insulin resistance will prevent fat loss]
- sufficient rest / not too much stress, as too much stress leads the nervous system into fight or flight mode & carb craving and poor food choices
- quality sleep (or the system can switch into fight or flight mode)

- movement / activity levels to increase expenditure & muscle mass, (as increased muscle mass will mean increased energy requirements)
- adequate liver and thyroid function
- genetic predisposition can impact, but can be expressed differently with a change in lifestyle and approach to nutrition / activity / sleep / stress.
- by limiting anxiety and emotional stress (this will tend to put nervous system into fight or /flight)
- for peri / post-menopausal women, who can become oestrogen deficient, HRT can help. (There is a tiny amount of oestrogen in fat cells and so the brain detects this and wants to hold onto the fat {even though the oestrogen in those fat cells has no benefit!})

Whilst fat loss is dependent on some calorie deficit, it is also affected by a whole range of other factors, too – so don't let anyone ever tell you it is solely about input and output, as that is super-simplistic and totally inaccurate! I should like to refer you to the following authors and titles if you wish to gain a more in-depth understanding of all the factors that impact weight loss (and overall health):

Unlocking the Keto Code, by Dr Stephen Gundry;
The Gut Balance Revolution, by Dr Gerard Mullins;

Rushing Woman Syndrome, *Accidentally Overweight* and *The Invisible Load*, by Dr Libby Weaver;

It's Not A Diet, and Hack Your Hormones, by Davinia Taylor;

Change Your Brain, Change Your Body, by Dr Daniel Amen;
The Glucose Revolution, by Jessie Inchauspe;

Switch on your Brain, by Dr Caroline Leaf; and
The Obesity Code, by Dr Jason Fung.

APPENDIX 2

Interesting Facts about Alcohol

1. Alcoholism vs Alcohol Misuse Disorder

The statement I am about to make is a bold one and some will not agree and that is perfectly reasonable as we will have different perspectives on this....here goes... No one is an alcoholic. "What?!" I hear you shout, "You can't say that! It's just not true!"

Well, I invite you to reflect on this possibility and let me know, when you see a new baby for the first time whether they are an alcoholic or not? Or whether they have "come into the world naked"! (Annie Grace, *This Naked Mind*)

I found the term 'alcoholic' unhelpful because it associates a dependency on a substance – whether psychological or physical – with a person's identity. However, a person's identity is unique. If they had never consumed alcohol, they could not be dependent on it. Moreover, we do not mix any other substance misuse with a person's identity: there are no heroin-oholics or crack-oholics. Alcohol Misuse Disorder feels like better terminology. That all said, if people find it helpful to "self-identify" because it enables them to navigate their freedom, then there is no judgement of this. I simply offer "alcohol misuse disorder" as an alternative, to help remove the stigma and shame so often associated with alcohol addiction.

2. Alcohol Misuse Disorder symptoms (AMD)

AMD can be mild, moderate or severe, based on the number of symptoms you experience. Signs and symptoms may include:

- Being unable to limit the amount of alcohol you drink
- Wanting to cut down on how much you drink or making unsuccessful attempts to do so
- Spending a lot of time drinking, getting alcohol or recovering from alcohol use (aka nights out on a session)
- Developing a tolerance to alcohol so you need more to feel its effect, or you have a reduced effect from the same amount
- Feeling a strong craving or urge to drink alcohol
- Failing to fulfil major obligations at work, school or home, due to repeated alcohol use
- Continuing to drink alcohol even though you know it's causing physical, social or interpersonal problems
- Giving up, or reducing hobbies, social and work activities
- Using alcohol in situations where it's not safe, such as when driving or swimming
- Experiencing withdrawal symptoms – such as nausea, sweating and shaking – when you don't drink, or drinking to avoid these symptoms

The scalar applied to assess where one is on the scale,[73] is as follows:

- MILD 2-3
- MODERATE 4-5
- SEVERE 6 or MORE

3. What happens when we drink alcohol

Blood / alcohol level rises > artificial stimulation of pleasure hormone > dopamine in the brain the first 20-30 mins, then it falls quite steeply as brain releases a counter measure > Dynorphin opioid called dynorphin, which is generally responsible for dysphoria > a profound sense of unease or dissatisfaction, which then causes a person to reach for the next drink once the initial "buzz" subsides.

The brain is very clever and when we engage in regularly exposing our brains to alcohol, it prepares its response to mitigate. It can even anticipate this if you become a regular drinker and equally biochemically it is why, in the 'habit' space, we will often want to consume alcohol at a similar time each day… Only now, the brain is prepared meaning we need more to stimulate the pleasure centre (in the brain).

With enough over exposure to both quantity and frequency, it becomes a habit. This is because we are creatures of habit and also because the biochemistry, in relation to addiction, is commencing and escalating over time.

4. It is estimated that only 10% of people with an alcohol use disorder are physically dependant

This means that 90% of people dependent in some way on alcohol, are not physically addicted and most of them have good jobs, with many doing well in life. Yep – you heard me right. Most people who have some dependance on the substance are the people we know and see every day: our work colleagues, friends, gym buddies, drinking pals and church friends. No sector of society lacks individuals on the 'increasing alcohol consumption trajectory', whether they are mildly or moderately dependent. I share that, because the typical image of someone using alcohol in the "mild", "moderate", or "severe" disorder spaces, are associated with the very small number who are in the 10% group. They are often in and out of work, in or out of treatment centres and commonly depicted by the person sitting on the park bench, or the street corners, seemingly homeless. The truth is, these individuals are a small proportion of people with a dependance on alcohol.

5. Impact of alcohol on our body and brain

Here follows some research results regarding impact:

1. It is believed to be one of the main causes of seven types of cancer (Bowel cancer, Breast cancer, Laryngeal cancer [voice box], Liver cancer, Mouth cancer, Oesophageal cancer [food pipe] and Pharyngeal cancer [upper throat]. See this website for an example, https://www.healthline.com/health-/yes-drinking-alcohol-can-increase-your-risk-of-breast-cancer)
2. Raises breast cancer risk for women by 7-16% (not dependent on quantity consumed)
3. It's a stimulant and a depressant
4. Impact on the Liver: The liver has to produce a more toxic substance than the body to get rid of the toxin in alcohol and whilst it's dealing with alcohol, it isn't dealing efficiently with its main function (to remove toxins from what you are eating)
5. Impact on the brain in terms of memory / brain function (like putting a virus in your computer)

6. Takes fourteen days for the body to fully eliminate it from your 'biochemistry' which is why the first fourteen days when taking a break can be the most challenging
7. LATEST research states there is no safe amount of alcohol consumption
(visit https://www.bbc.co.uk/news/health-45283401)

Bibliography and Further Reading Recommendations

1. This Naked Mind - Annie Grace
2. The Alcohol Experiment - Annie Grace
3. This Naked Mind Institute (TNMI) Coaching Manual - Annie Grace
4. The Ruthless Elimination of Hurry - John Mark Comer
5. Celebration of Discipline - Richard Foster
6. Definition of Stress - Medical Encyclopaedia
7. The Obesity Code - Dr Jason Fung
8. The Gut Balance Revolution - Dr Gerard Mullins
9. Rushing Woman Syndrome - Dr Libby Weaver
10. Accidentally Overweight - Dr Libby Weaver
11. The Invisible Load - Dr Libby Weaver
12. It's Not A Diet - Davinia Taylor
13. Change Your Brain, Change Your Body - Dr Daniel Amen
14. The Glucose Revolution - Jessie Inchauspe
15. Switch On Your Brain - Dr Caroline Leaf
16. Unlocking the Keto Code – Dr Stephen Gundry

Online resources for further reading

To read John Sutherland's blog: https://www.polfed.org/news/blogs/2021/blog-every-police-officer-has-their-scars/

For more about cortisol: https://www.positivepause.co.uk/all-blogs/why-does-cortisol-affect-women-in-midlife-7-easy-steps-to-balance-cortisol-in-menopause

To learn more on Sleep Foundation: https://www.sleepfoundation.org/stages-of-sleep/deep-sleep

For information about *Lumen* – their mission and origins: https://www.lumen.me/about

For more information about Infinite8Wellbeing – email sara@infinite8wellbeing.com

Endnotes

1. This Naked Mind. Find freedom from alcohol. Visit *www.thisnakedmind.com.*
2. TNMI - This Naked Mind Institute - this is the coaching programme delivered by Annie Grace and her team from This Naked Mind [*www.thisnakedmind.com*]. The programme equips coaches to become effective in coaching people using a methodology based on hope, relationship and tactics to enable the client to be able to change thoughts and beliefs in order to change behaviours.
3. Lumen is a device which is a metabolic tracker and provides 'real time' metabolic feedback. This will be explored in detail in chapter 6 and further information is available via my affiliate link: *www.lumen.me/=*
4. Supraventricular Tachycardia (or SVT), is an abnormally fast heart rhythm due to improper electrical activity in the upper part of the heart.
5. Rest-day in lieu. This is a day off that has been accrued for working a day not rostered to work, usually as a result of a period of on-call duty outside of normal working hours or a special operation, or previously cancelled rest day, which might have occurred due to operational requirements.
6. This Naked Mind Intensive: A three-month coaching programme to support an individual to change their relationship with alcohol and take back control by means of changing thoughts and beliefs, which ultimately leads to changed desires. It means a person is not relying on willpower, but rather can choose not to drink, or to drink moderately without any sense, or fear, of missing out.
7. The Live Alcohol Experiment is a 30-day programme where participants plan to take a break from consuming alcohol: consisting of a daily coaching video, a community platform and live coaching for an hour, with an opportunity for Q & A. It is the live version of The Live Alcohol Experiment, which is available

online via *https://learn.thisnakedmind.com/the-alcohol-experiment-registration*. It is a flagship programme developed by Annie Grace and *This Naked Mind*.

8. 'Process' - this was the term we used to describe summons reports: We would prepare for summary offences - offences which are heard at the magistrates court and most often related to traffic law infringements, though not exclusively. It was the probationer's bread-and-butter in their early police service.
9. Green cards: In Greater Manchester Police, the summons reports were handwritten on green coloured report cards, hence 'green cards'.
10. The standard response car course was a three-week driver training course which, if successful, qualified an officer to drive over the speed limit to 999 / urgent incidents that required a response from police in less than ten minutes. It enabled the driver to activate the emergency equipment on the police vehicle - blue lights and two-tone sirens. It did not make an officer eligible to pursue offending vehicles. (This necessitated a four-week more advanced driving course.)
11. 'A relief' - one of the five shifts at Stratford who rotated with four others, over a 24/7 shift pattern of early shifts, late shifts and night shifts.
12. Shouts - open calls 'over the air' for a police unit to respond to an incident that had been reported via 999 or the non-urgent call line.
13. 'Over the air' - communications made by the operators in the control room to deploy police officers to incidents.
14. Response - this is a key uniform policing role primarily focused on responding to immediate and urgent calls from members of the public.
15. Corporate Development - this was a department in Greater Manchester Police which was responsible for strategy, direction and improvement within work at an organisational level.
16. David Lloyd Leisure - David Lloyd Leisure is a group of fitness and leisure clubs, often with racket sports facilities, founded by tennis player David Lloyd. Details of the club franchise can be found at *https://www.davidlloyd.co.uk*
17. Operations' Chief Inspector - this was a uniform role where I was responsible for all of the uniformed response policing and operational plans for pre-planned operations, sometimes supporting other departments.
18. Critical incidents as defined in policing are "any incident where the effectiveness of the police response is likely to have a significant impact on the confidence of the victim, their family and/or the community." - College

of Policing - *https://www.college.police.uk/app/critical-incident-management/introduction-and-types-critical-incidents*

19. Police Treatment Centres - *https://www.thepolicetreatmentcentres.org*
20. West Midlands Police Benevolent Fund website – https://wmpben.co.uk
21. Cortisol – "a steroid hormone that your adrenal glands, the endocrine glands on top of your kidneys, produce and release. Cortisol affects several aspects of your body and mainly helps regulate your body's response to stress." Cited from Cleveland Clinic, *Cortisol: What It Is, Function, Symptoms & Levels.* Retrieved from https://clevelandclinic.org
22. Force Executive Team Gold Commander - this was an Assistant Chief Constable who was on an 'on-call' duty rota for operational oversight of the entire Force area.
23. Les Mills RPM Indoor Cycle, is one of the Les Mills branded cycle fitness programmes.
24. 'Prophetic' - this is a Christian term derived from the word prophecy. Prophecy is one of the nine gifts of the Holy Spirit described by the apostle Paul, particularly in his letter to the church at Corinth (found in 1 Corinthians chapter 12 and chapter 14, in the New Testament]). It relates to the activity of someone hearing the voice of Creator God and speaking out to one (or more) what they understand and believe God to be saying. 'Prophesying' is the action [verb] of that speaking and the 'prophecy' is the content of what is said, or has been said [the abstract noun]. The 'prophetic' is a colloquialism with the church to describe the entirety of this context.
25. John Sutherland. Blog: "Every Police Officer Has Their Scars". Posted 12th May 2021. Read the whole article at *https://www.polfed.org/news/blogs/2021/blog-every-police-officer-has-their-scars/*
26. Wake up and smell the coffee is an injunction to face up to reality or face the facts, an Americanism first cited in the Chicago Daily Tribune 18 January 1943. It is not known who coined the expression the expression but the Anne Landers advice column in the Chicago Sun-Times popularised it during the 1960s. Sourced from www.idiomorigins.org/origin/wake-up-and-smell-the-coffee
27. GP - General medical practitioner - in the UK, this is a person's local doctor, accessed via a local surgery.
28. ECG test – 'electrocardiogram'. An ECG is a simple and useful test that records the rhythm, rate and electrical activity of your heart.
29. Turkey is now known as Türkiye (pron. Tur-key-YAY)

30. A.D.A.M. Medical Encyclopedia. "Stress and your health". Part of the National Library of Medicine. To read the full article, go to https://medlineplus.gov/ency/article/003211.htm
31. The pressure performance curve - this is a bell-shaped trajectory that charts the relationship between pressure and performance. You may know this curve as the "Stress Curve". They are one and the same, but it's more useful to think of 'pressure' instead of 'stress', because stress, for most people, is a negative experience.
32. Metabolic syndrome: A group of health conditions leading to increased risk of heart diseases and related problems.
33. Dr. Libby Weaver. (2011). *Rushing Woman's Syndrome: The impact of a never-ending to-do list on our health.* © Little Green Frog Publishing.
34. Sleep hygiene - these are important considerations to support and promote healthy sleep, in terms of preparation for sleep and creating the best environment for rest.
35. Garmin watch – a fitness / lifestyle watch developed by Garmin. To find out about the Garmin Fenix watch, head along to https://www.garmin.com/en-GB/p/735520
36. Heart rate variability [HRV] - Heart rate variability is where the amount of time between your heartbeats fluctuates slightly. Even though these fluctuations are undetectable except with specialised devices, they can still indicate current or future health problems, including heart conditions and mental health issues like anxiety and depression. Here is a recommended article to read on HRV: *https://www.whoop.com/en-gb/thelocker/heart-rate-variability-hrv/*
37. Danielle Pacheco, Staff Writer for Sleep Foundation. (2022). *Deep Sleep: How much Do You Need?* Updated March 11, 2022. Medically reviewed by Dr. Abhinav Singh, Sleep Physician. Retrieved from https://www.sleepfoundation.org/stages-of-sleep/deep-sleep
38. Jay Summer, Staff Writer for Sleep Foundation. (2022). *What is REM Sleep and How Much Do You Need? > Why Is REM Sleep Important?* Updated April 26, 2022. Medically reviewed by Dr. Abhinav Singh, Sleep Physician. Retrieved from https://www.sleepfoundation.org/stages-of-sleep/rem-sleep
39. There are a number of contenders as to why the 'day of rest' changed from a Saturday to Sunday in the Christian Church, during the era of the Roman Empire. One of which is how the biblical narrative speaks of Jesus Christ rising from the dead on the "first day of the week" (Mark 16:9). Acts 20:7 and

1 Corinthians 16:2 in *The Bible* appears to show the early Jewish Christians meeting on a Sunday, (the "first day of the week"), as supposed to the traditional Saturday. However, there could be other reasons why, including a time of persecution the Jews suffered, which took place during the first century, causing Christians to air an element of 'disassociation' with them for fear of their own lives.

40. Martin Luther, O.S.A.; 10 November 1483 – February 18, 1546. A German professor of theology, composer, priest, monk, and a seminal figure in the protestant reformation. His quote: "I am so busy now that if I did not spend three hours each ..." | Citatis. Full URL for quote is: https://citatis.com/a13178/169f52/#:~:text=Martin%20Luther%20Quotes%20I%20am%20so%20busy%20now,could%20not%20get%20through%20the%20day.%20Martin%20Luther

41. Matthew Walker, Why We Sleep: Unlocking the Power of Sleep and Dreams. Quote by Matthew Walker: "Sleep is the single most effective thing we can..." (goodreads.com). First published by Scribner, September 28, 2017. Matthew Walker is a British scientist and professor of neuroscience and psychology at the University of California, Berkeley. His research focuses on the impact of sleep on human health and disease. Previously, he was a professor of psychiatry at Harvard Medical School.

42. Maria Fox featured in *Midlife Fitness Files* of the Daily Telegraph https://www.telegraph.co.uk/health-fitness/body/lost-35-stone-seven-months-changing-one-thing-routine/ and "The healthy habit that helped us lose weight, according to 12 midlifers" (telegraph.co.uk)

43. To find out more about Lumen and read their mission statement, visit *https://www.lumen.me/about*

44. Respiratory exchange rate or ratio: The respiratory exchange ratio (RER) is the ratio between the metabolic production of carbon dioxide (CO_2) and the uptake of oxygen (O_2). This is proven to be a key indicator of what energy source (free fatty acids or carbohydrates) the metabolism is using in the moment, for its requirements.

45. Ketones - are a type of chemical that your liver produces when it breaks down fats. Your body uses ketones for energy typically during fasting, long periods of exercise, or when you don't have as many carbohydrates. You can have low levels of ketones in your blood without it being a problem. For more information on the subject, visit: https://www.diabetes.org.uk/guide-to-diabetes/managing-your-diabetes/ketones-and-diabetes

46. VO2 max and cardio respiratory fitness – this is defined as the maximum or optimum rate at which the heart, lungs, and muscles can effectively use oxygen during exercise, used as a way of measuring a person's individual aerobic capacity. Cardiorespiratory fitness (CRF) refers to the ability of the circulatory and respiratory systems to supply oxygen to skeletal muscles during sustained physical activity. Scientists and researchers use CRF to assess the functional capacity of the respiratory and cardiovascular systems.
47. Grace, Annie. (2018). *"The Alcohol Experiment: A 30-Day Alcohol-Free Challenge to Interrupt Your Habits and Help You Take Control."* Published by Penguin Random House USA, 31st December, 2018.
48. Anticoagulant medication - these are medicines that help prevent blood clots. They're given to people at a high risk of getting clots, to reduce their chances of developing.
49. To find out about Circle by DNAfit, visit https://www.dnafit.com/about
50. Genetic expression - this is highly scientific and I recommend researching on the internet! In relation to its use in this book, it is simply referring to the fact that though our genetic make-up and origins, predisposition might be 'set'. The subsequent expressions can be impacted by thinking and lifestyle choices. I recommend Dr Caroline Leaf's book on this subject, titled Switch on your brain (see Bibliography). In my case, genetic propensity towards being overweight and having a larger waist with stress related obesity, have been impacted by lifestyle choices, which have now resulted in the opposite expression. I am now slim, with good average stress levels and elimination of obesity. Whilst I may have the disposition towards more negative factors, my *choices* have enabled me to express differently.
51. Gut microbiome: The human digestive-tract associated microbes are referred to as the gut microbiome. The human gut microbiome and its role in both health and disease has been the subject of extensive research, establishing its involvement in human metabolism, nutrition, physiology, and immune function.
52. Adrenal Function: The adrenal glands produce hormones that help regulate your metabolism, immune system, blood pressure, response to stress and other essential functions. Adrenal glands are composed of two parts (the cortex and the medulla), which are each responsible for producing different endocrines.
53. To find out about Healthpath, the Functional Medicine company, visit www.healthpath.com

54. Gut dysbiosis - Gut dysbiosis is a broad term that can be defined as the imbalance of gut microbiota associated with an unhealthy outcome. Dysbiosis involves the loss of beneficial microbial input or signal and an expansion of pathogenic microbes (pathobionts).
55. To learn more gut microbiome, I recommend reading this article by healthline: *https://www.healthline.com/nutrition/gut-microbiome-and-health#TOC_TITLE_HDR_4*
56. DHEA - Dehydroepiandrosterone (DHEA) is an endocrine that your body naturally produces in the adrenal gland. DHEA helps produce other hormones, including testosterone and estrogen. Natural DHEA levels peak in early adulthood and then slowly fall as you age.
57. Dr. Caroline Leaf. *Switch On Your Brain: The Key to Peak Happiness, Thinking and Health.* Visit her online store at www.drleaf.com
58. 'Managed return-to-work' - this is a transitional process for officers returning to work after an extended period, where they will build up their hours and duties gradually over an agreed period of time as directed by medical practitioners.
59. People and Organisational Development - this a headquarters 'people' function in West Midlands Police that governs all aspects of HR.
60. Recruitment Uplift Programme - this is a national government funded initiative established to support the recruitment of 20,000 additional police officers over three years, by March 2023.
61. Recruitment Ambassadors - this was an internal initiative that I developed to support the Recruitment Uplift Programme by enlisting officers and staff already in West Midlands Police, to reach out to potential new recruits and encourage them to submit an application to become a police officer; particularly focusing on under-represented groups.
62. Summer Academy – was an initiative to provide a behind-the-scenes experience for young black people from a local school. They spent three days with us learning about what really goes on in policing through a series of workshops, interviews, a case study and by watching some of the specialist teams in action (e.g., search, dogs, drones).
63. Humans of WMP - these are internal articles/blogs of West Midlands Police, where employees share their personal/professional journeys to encourage others.
64. NPU - Neighbourhood Policing Unit

65. The 'Four Pillars' as quoted by the author, are Nutrition, Movement, Sleep and Stress Management.
66. Carpe diem, (Latin: "pluck the day" or "seize the day"). A phrase used by the Roman poet Horace to express the idea that one should enjoy life while one can. Visit www.britannica.com/topic/carpe-diem
67. 'Turned out to a job' - this is police slang for attending an incident usually when an officer had returned to the police station to do some administration, or take a refreshment break.
68. Circadian rhythms are "24-hour cycles that are part of the body's internal clock, running in the background to carry out essential functions and processes. One of the most important and well-known circadian rhythm is the sleep-wake cycle." Taken from Sleep Foundation. Website: www.sleepfoundation.org/circadian-rhythm
69. The Latin "Scientia potential est" literally means, "knowledge is power". It is an aphorism commonly attributed to Sir Francis Bacon, written for the first time (according to Wikipedia) in the 1668 version of *Leviathan* by Thomas Hobbes.
70. The first written source of an aphorism stating the connection that "where [through knowledge] there is power, great responsibility follows", is in the gospel of Luke, chapter 12 verse 48. Jesus of Nazareth is pen by the author as saying, "For everyone to whom much is given, of him shall much be required; and of him to whom men entrust much, they will require and demand all the more." (Amplified Bible, Classic Edition {AMPC}). Other prominent leaders, such as Winston Churchill and Teddy Roosevelt, have made similar statements. It also featured in the 1962 comic book of Spider-Man.
71. TFC - Tactical Firearms Commander - is a police commander who develops and oversees the implementation of a tactical plan required in the deployment of armed police officers, in a police operation.
72. For quotes around this saying, visit https://quotessayings.net/topics/scars-wounds
73. To find out where an alcohol dependant is on the associated scale, visit this website: https://patient.info/doctor/alcohol-use-disorders-identification-test-audit